THE BEST GRAIN-FREE FAMILY MEALS ON THE PLANET

THE BEST GRAIN-FREE FAMILY MEALS ON THE PLANET

Make Grain-Free Breakfasts, Lunches, and Dinners
Your Whole Family Will Love
with More Than 170 Delicious Recipes

Laura Fuentes
Founder of MOMables.com

FAIR WINDS

Quarto is the authority on a wide range of topics.

Quarto educates, entertains and enriches the lives of our readers—enthusiasts and lovers of hands-on living.

www.QuartoKnows.com

First published in the United States of America in 2016 by
Fair Winds Press, an imprint of
Quarto Publishing Group USA Inc.
100 Cummings Center
Suite 406-L
Beverly, Massachusetts 01915-6101
Telephone: (978) 282-9590
Fax: (978) 283-2742
QuartoKnows.com
Visit our blogs at QuartoKnows.com

20 19 18 17 16   1 2 3 4 5

ISBN: 978-1-59233-719-4

Digital edition published in 2016
eISBN: 978-1- 63159-164-8

Library of Congress Cataloging-in-Publication Data available.

Design: Carol Holtz
Page Layout: *tabula rasa* graphic design
Photography: Alison Bickel Photography
Illustrations: iStock and Shutterstock

Printed in China

The information in this book is for educational purposes only. It is not intended to replace the advice of a physician or medical practitioner. Please see your health-care provider before beginning any new health program

To my husband, Eric, and kids, Sofia, Alex, and Gabriel,
for helping me stretch my imagination in the kitchen.

CONTENTS

INTRODUCTION

I've struggled with digestive issues as long as I can remember. In my twenties, I mostly ate a low-fat and whole-grain diet. My protein came from low-fat dairy items, many of which contained artificial sweeteners and unidentifiable ingredients.

I ate foods that were labeled "natural" and "whole grain" without questioning the ingredients in fine print on the labels. I went through a period when I gave up eating meat altogether in favor of only soy-derived proteins. My digestive system didn't like that either.

I felt sluggish, often bloated after meals, and, to be honest, I wasn't that excited about eating food. And then, I had emergency gallbladder surgery at the young age of twenty-four. Complications left me feeling lucky to have woken up from the surgery at all.

Immediately, I removed all fried foods from my diet, added lean animal proteins back in, and limited processed ingredients. I felt "fine"... but not great.

In addition, I suffered from terrible seasonal allergies that got progressively worse over time and with each pregnancy. During my third pregnancy, I would wake up in the middle of the night, barely able to breathe and not able to take any additional medication.

Soon after delivery, my newborn Gabriel seemed irritable each time I nursed. I had two other kids who were gassy and colicky, but this little dude seemed unhappier than the first two.

Doing a little research, I learned that gluten and dairy proteins passed down in breast milk are often culprits of digestive issues in infants. Within a few days, I eliminated all gluten and dairy from my diet and Gabriel seemed to respond really well. Coincidentally, I lost nearly all the pregnancy weight in about eight weeks, not eight months as with the first two kids (something shocking to me since Gabriel was my third C-section).

I noticed a significant improvement after a couple of months so I decided to continue with the modified diet restrictions a little longer. However, I found myself making multiple meals for my family and I fell off the wagon often. Drastic dietary changes are never easy and being unprepared was my downfall. I was also bored with food because I ate the same things all the time.

After nearly a year, when I weaned Gabriel from breast-feeding, I returned to eating "normally." With three kids and a new business, I didn't have time to be a short-order cook (and neither do you, I'm sure!). Unfortunately for me, however, my allergy and digestive symptoms returned.

I'll continue about my own journey in the next couple of pages. However, I feel it's important to share a little about the other two people who have been instrumental in the creation of this book: my two sons Gabriel and Alex. You'll see how their stories weave into mine and you'll understand why a grain-free diet (and "nearly Paleo") works best for my entire family—and may do wonders for your family, too.

Gabriel: The Dairy-Free Kid

Gabriel (my third child) was born a good eater. But while he was constantly hungry, he spit up occasionally and was very (very) gassy. When he was one month old, I removed dairy and gluten from my diet to help him digest my breast milk proteins better. He did great like this until my milk supply wasn't enough; I was working full time without the ability to pump as much as I needed to, and I had to supplement with formula.

Finding a formula that he could tolerate was a bit of a challenge, but I settled on one where the milk proteins are broken down for easier digestion. For the most part he was a healthy baby but, around the seventh month, he began getting colds and sinus infections often. The pediatrician attributed his symptoms to "allergies" and the older two siblings bringing germs home from school. He was put on a daily dose of allergy medicine to control the symptoms, but he still suffered.

At eight months, I introduced whole-milk baby yogurt (one per day or every other day). At first, he tolerated them well and was a happy baby after his meals. Soon though, his colds came more often and stayed longer. When he was ten months old, his chest congestion was so bad for three weeks that the pediatrician thought he had pneumonia (a chest X-ray ruled it out but confirmed a lot of mucus buildup). I was constantly hooking him up to the nebulizer because he couldn't breathe. The poor baby was miserable and sick for about two months. At the same time, he had four ear infections between month six (shortly after we introduced formula) to right before turning one.

When Gabriel turned one, he entered "school" (daycare) three days per week. He was sick nearly every week for two straight months. Everyone assured me this was normal and that he needed to get used to the germs and build up his immunity; the pediatrician, again, said she was sure it sounded like pneumonia (and again the chest X-ray ruled it out). At this point, I'd had enough with my baby being sick for seven months straight! I was tired of the allergy medicine, antibiotics, breathing treatments, X-rays, ER visits, and constant doctor checkups.

I began looking at alternative medicine for help and I often read the suggestion to eliminate dairy to improve congestion and allergy issues. I decided I would eliminate Gabriel's sixteen ounces (475 ml) of whole (organic) milk and the daily yogurt from his diet. Within one week, all of his congestion went away. A few days later I stopped giving him his daily dose of allergy medicine (after consulting the pediatrician) and have not given it to him since.

He can now tolerate some dairy products, such as sharp Cheddar cheese, kefir, and the occasional whole-milk yogurt; however, if he consumes too much dairy in a short period of time, his congestion symptoms return.

Alex: The Gluten-Free Kid

When Alex (my second child) was born, he wasn't the biggest baby on the block. Naturally, he gained weight but he remained consistently in the fifth to tenth percentile for his age. Our pediatrician always suggested supplemental options to help him gain weight and "thrive," but I never took him up on it. Alex was consistently growing and gaining weight; he just remained at the bottom of the chart. He is slim, to say the least.

As a baby, Alex nursed well and I didn't have to change anything in my diet for him to digest my breast milk well. Eventually, he transitioned to an organic formula and ate a variety of foods. The one thing we had trouble with was his stools. Since he was a baby, he was often constipated and my heart would ache seeing him "push" as an infant.

I cloth-diapered him and, by the time he was seven months old, I would sit him on the potty so he would be in an ergonomic posture to ease the passing of the stool. Needless to say, he was potty trained to poop on the potty at around fourteen months.

Of course, with solid foods came solid stools. He ate most foods but never seemed to have a huge appetite. The pediatrician continued to suggest we give him plenty of liquid and continue his whole-grain and high-fiber diet.

One day, when Alex was two, we were at a birthday party inside a very busy bounce house arcade when he asked to go make "ca-ca" (our word for poop). Dragging the stroller and his four-year-old sister with me, I sat him on a (paper-lined) toilet and let him do his business. What happened next was the beginning of the reality that my son had stomach issues. As he pushed his stools he began to cry—a little at first, and then screaming. I remember holding him tight and thinking to myself that something was wrong. When he was finished and I wiped his little butt, I saw blood. I'm not talking about a little blood on the toilet paper, I mean a lot. When I finally got him clean and lifted him off the toilet and I looked inside the bowl, the water was red.

I rushed him to the doctor's office. Upon a visual inspection, the doctor said he didn't see any external hemorrhoids and that, perhaps, his stool was hard and he tore an internal hemorrhoid as he pushed. He also suggested we give him more water, continue his high-fiber diet, and see a pediatric gastroenterologist the following week. For the next couple of days, we continued to see blood in his stool but never as a gush of blood like the first time.

Our appointment with the gastro was better than with our pediatrician. He suggested we put Alex on a high dose of stool softener for a month to allow any tearing or bruising to heal inside his intestinal wall. He said that if we continued to see blood in his stool after two weeks, Alex needed a colonoscopy to determine the cause of the bleeding.

Luckily for Alex, the bleeding stopped and the colonoscopy wasn't necessary. Over time, he went from the kid who ate nearly everything as a toddler to a very picky eater who would eat only a few selected foods. At four years of age, I could count the number of foods he ate on two hands. Bathroom trips continued to be less than pleasant.

Twice, from four and a half years to almost six, I took him to the emergency room with stomach pains that were so bad you'd think something was tearing his insides. An abdominal X-ray confirmed he had impacted bowels and possibly irritated intestines. The doctor recommended we give him more fiber, more water, and fresh fruit.

Unfortunately, my very picky eater lived on a diet filled mostly with whole wheat and dairy. The fruits and veggies that were snuck in and dinnertime were often an issue. He was never hungry. He never wanted to eat breakfast, lunch was barely eaten, and dinner was a fight. My mom joked that my son lived on air and water alone.

I reached the peak of my frustration three months after I went grain-free. Frustrated with my son's constant food struggles, lack of appetite, little help from doctors besides the reassuring, "some kids are just hard of stool," and constant nagging from my family, I decided to take matters into my own hands to see if a similar diet might work for him.

The day after his sixth birthday, I explained to him that he was going on a gluten-free diet. Meaning, we were going to work together to find foods that he would eat that didn't have regular flour so his stomach would stop hurting.

The first week was a little tough and we had a couple of "I didn't know I wasn't supposed to eat that" instances. After that, he was actually pretty receptive to some of his new foods and slowly began to try new foods. For two weeks I added probiotic capsules to his morning glass of milk to help restore his gut (he now takes them almost daily).

After the second week of Alex's strict gluten-free diet, many of his bathroom issues disappeared. (And since then, he is now "regular" and no longer finds it painful to go.) After three weeks, he gained one pound (454 g). His skin became brighter and the dark circles under his eyes practically disappeared. After a month, he became his own advocate and began telling people that he eats a special gluten-free diet because his stomach used to hurt all the time.

Now, I make time each weekend to bake treats and re-create some of our favorite staples for him. Since he still doesn't get all the calories he needs for the day, he often eats a bowl of Nut Clusters (page 64) before bed. Many of the breakfast recipes and treats in this book were developed for Alex, so you can imagine his excitement to find them in Mommy's cookbook and to share them with you.

The Rest of the Family

My husband and oldest daughter can eat a traditional diet. In other words, they can eat whatever they want and feel fine—lucky them!

If we eat any type of grain at our house, it's always gluten-free. It's a lot easier for me to make one grain for everyone, although I'd say that most of our meals are grain-free. It's just easier that way. Of course, on occasion, when we eat out or attend social gatherings, my husband and daughter eat traditional foods.

Grain-Free Is a *Lifestyle*

The reality is that some of my family feels better without grains and dairy. I've felt so good for so long that my body tells me (nearly immediately) when I've eaten something I shouldn't have.

Alex has varied reactions to gluten consumption, from going to the bathroom almost immediately after eating a slice of regular pizza, to going several days without using the bathroom, to extreme irritability and mood swings a few hours later. I never know what will happen after gluten consumption but I can tell you that it nearly always takes almost a week of being very strict with his diet for him to get back to normal.

As for Gabriel, just when I think he's outgrown his dairy symptoms, they return. While he doesn't drink cow's milk, he sometimes eats ice cream. Boy oh boy is that a mistake if he's already had any dairy that day. Stuffiness returns full force and, if I don't catch it in time, meaning he continues to have dairy, he gets a cold or sinus infection.

As you can see, our family has a range of food intolerances—something your family may struggle with as well. For us, eating grain-free and nearly dairy-free is a choice we make daily for our health, and I'm so glad we do! The learning curve can be steep, but once you're on the right track, you'll be amazed at how good you feel.

CHAPTER 1
LIVING A GRAIN-FREE LIFESTYLE WITH KIDS

NOTHING IS IMPOSSIBLE in the kitchen—
with the right recipe inspiration. And that includes
grain-free meals! With a little know-how
and preparation, you'll quickly be on your way to
creating meals your kids will not only eat,
but will also look forward to!

What to Expect from This Book

When I shared this book with Kelly, a really good friend of mine who is also a nutritionist, she asked why I didn't call this book *Paleo for Kids*. I explained that I didn't want to limit the creativity of the book and that there would be a handful of recipes that contain beans and non-Paleo-approved items such as dairy.

While our journeys to a grain-free diet might be different, we all have the same need for grain-free recipes. The recipes in this book are the ones I feed my own family, and I'm proud to share them with you.

GLUTEN-FREE-ONLY DIETS

I realize that some of you might be avoiding gluten only and purchased this book for inspiration and to expand the variety of foods in your repertoire. If you can tolerate things such as rice, for instance, you can use that instead in recipes that call for cauliflower rice (page 145). You'll also be able to use gluten-free bread instead of the grain-free Blender Bread (page 40). Overall, however, I have created this to be of value to you even if you don't follow a 100 percent grain-free diet.

DAIRY-FREE DIETS

Nearly all recipes in this book contain a substitute, or were developed with dairy-free alternatives, such as canned coconut milk or almond milk.

If you can tolerate dairy, use regular cow's milk where almond milk might be called for and half-and-half or cream where coconut milk is listed.

NUT-FREE DIETS

Some recipes contain nuts and seeds. Unlike many other paleo and grain-free books, however, I don't rely on nuts and seeds to fill the recipe count. The recipes that require almond flour or whole nuts will always have an Allergy Substitution provided. And, for your convenience, I also show you how to make my No-Nut Flour (page 32).

I felt really strongly about making sure that nearly all recipes included in the book were tested with a nut-free option, not just for your family's safety but also for the safety of other children with severe nut allergies around your child. Nut allergies are no joke so I wanted to make sure you had a good alternative should you want to make the recipe without nuts.

ALL OTHER ALLERGY RESTRICTIONS

I can't possibly account for all the different individual-ingredient allergies out there, but I encourage you to make changes as needed. If you or your child is allergic to shellfish, for example, please do not make the handful of recipes in this book that include that ingredient. Or, if you can't tolerate berries, substitute another fruit.

The recipes in this book are designed to guide you in your journey to a cleaner, allergy-free, grain-free diet. I hope they inspire you to add variety to your family's meals as much as they've helped me with mine.

Facing a New Diagnosis

A recent diagnosis of an autoimmune disease or food allergy can crush anyone. Whether you are making dietary and lifestyle changes for yourself or because a family member was newly diagnosed, there will be many emotional ups and downs.

I receive hundreds of emails per week from new MOMables Community members who, like yourself, don't know where to begin. My advice is to arm yourself with knowledge, surround yourself with people who will support you in this difficult journey, and take it one change at a time.

There isn't much I can say to make this journey easier except that there are millions of people out there living with similar struggles and our attitudes toward the journey determine how happily we arrive at our destination.

Look at this diagnosis as an opportunity to embark on a new adventure, to take control of your and your family's health, and to make the kind of changes you've always wanted to make. *Easy?* No, but I promise it's worth it.

Grain-Free Basics

Eating grain-free does not have to be restrictive. Instead, I hope you see it as an opportunity to get creative with fresh and real foods. In time, making meals free of grains and other allergens will come naturally and you won't have to question constantly whether you can use a certain ingredient.

These recipes are meant to appeal to many eating styles. There is no one-size-fits-all recipe and, sometimes, you will have to make adjustments to fit your personal dietary needs. Unlike a Paleo diet, a grain-free diet can include dairy, legumes, white potatoes, and sugars. For the purpose of this book and to eat cleaner, I've omitted all soy products and refined sugars. You'll find coconut palm sugar in a few recipes, which has a similar texture to brown sugar.

To help you understand the ingredients I used in this book, consider the following guidelines:

Grain-Free at a Glance

EAT	LIMIT	AVOID
• Eggs • Fish • Lean meats • Vegetables, including root vegetables • Potatoes and sweet potatoes • Fruit • Nuts and seeds • Healthy oils and fats	• Dairy products, especially those high in sugars • Legumes and beans	• Grains and grain-based products • Corn • Refined or hydrogenated oils • Processed foods • Soy

The Grain-Free Kitchen and Pantry

For many of us, eating grain-free is not a temporary diet—it's a way of life. At the beginning, as with anything new, there will be a learning curve. For that reason, I've kept the recipes simple and similar to ones you've probably been eating prior to this dietary change. Hopefully, you—and moreover, your kids—don't feel as if your whole world's been turned upside down.

I realize that many of you have "mixed" households like mine, where some members have food restrictions while others don't. If that's the case, you are probably trying to make meals that accommodate some family members while making sure those that can eat without restrictions don't miss out. I've been there!

My experience with the "mixed" approach is that it is very time consuming. At the beginning, while you are learning to navigate food labels and ingredient lists, take your time. Learning to make new recipes, such as the ones in this book, to accommodate your dietary restrictions is what's most important.

After that, my hope is that you're able to transition your kitchen efforts to making one meal for everyone. For me, this was the simplest way to make meals with real and fresh ingredients without spending an eternity in the kitchen.

Easy Food Swaps

Pasta ▶	Spiralized sweet potatoes, spaghetti squash, or spiralized veggies
Rice ▶	Cauliflower rice (page 145)
Mashed white potatoes ▶	Mashed sweet potatoes, parsnips, or cauliflower (Mashed No-tatoes, page 200)
Milk ▶	Coconut milk, almond milk
Yogurt ▶	Canned coconut milk or cream
Sugar ▶	Coconut crystals, honey, maple syrup
Canola oil and vegetable oil ▶	Coconut oil, ghee
All-purpose flour ▶	Nut flours, No-Nut Flour (page 32), coconut flour
Soy sauce ▶	Coconut aminos

Grain-Free Pantry Essentials

Nuts and Seeds

Almonds
Cashews
Chia seeds
Flaxseed (whole or ground)
Pumpkin seeds
Sunflower seeds
Tahini
Walnuts

Healthy Cooking Fats

Avocado oil
Bacon fat (stored in a jar in the fridge)
Butter (if you can tolerate dairy)
Coconut oil
Extra-virgin olive oil (for salad dressings)
Ghee (clarified butter)
Olive oil (for roasting)

Baking Needs

Arrowroot powder
Baking powder (check the label to be sure it
    doesn't contain cornstarch, or see recipe,
    page 32)
Baking soda
Blanched almond flour or almond meal
Chocolate chips (check the ingredients of
    traditional brands for any possible allergens)
Coconut flour
Coconut milk, full fat (canned)
Coconut oil
Coconut palm sugar
Cream of tartar
Dried fruits
Nut flours
Raisins and dates (as natural sweeteners)
Seed flours (see No-Nut Flour, page 32)
Tapioca flour/starch
Unsweetened chocolate powder or cacao powder

Unsweetened coconut flakes and
    shredded coconut
Vanilla extract, pure
Vanilla powder

Natural Sweeteners

Coconut sugar
Dried fruits (no added sugar)
Honey
Maple syrup
Molasses
Pitted dates
Raisins

Condiments and Miscellaneous

Applesauce (unsweetened)
Chili sauce/hot sauce
Coconut aminos (a replacement for soy sauce)
Fish sauce
Ketchup (store bought or homemade)
Mustard
Olives
Pickles (check label for artificial colors)
Spices and seasoning blends
Tomato products (canned, diced tomatoes,
    sauce, paste)
Vinegars (apple cider, balsamic, white wine, and
    red wine)
Worcestershire sauce

REVAMPING THE PANTRY, STEP ONE: OUT WITH THE OLD

In the process of cleaning out your pantry and fridge, you are going to find cans that might be older than your firstborn. You'll find stale crackers, tons of open condiments with crusty edges, old cereal boxes, "cream-of" soups, pancake mixes, snacks with mile-long ingredient lists ... and more. Food items that are unopened and in edible condition (not expired) can be donated to a local food shelter or family in need. The only way to move forward and not be tempted, or worse, repeatedly have to say, "No, you can't have this" to one of your kids, is to get rid of it.

REVAMPING THE PANTRY, STEP TWO: IN WITH THE NEW

Restock your pantry with fresh, wholesome, real foods. Purchase foods that everyone in the family can eat and are not "off limits" to anyone.

To keep things simple, see the page opposite for basic staples that will get you started with the recipes in this book. Please note: There are many other ingredients in these categories that you may want to add; these cover the basic ingredients needed in this book and used in many other grain-free everyday recipes.

I purchase many of these items in bulk, both online and at a wholesale membership store. They are typically stored in my pantry, at room temperature, in airtight containers or sealed bags. Some, like raw nuts, nut flours, and nut butters, do best in the refrigerator or freezer (see below for shopping tips) to extend their shelf life.

Shopping: Where Is the Food?

You've probably heard it many times: when you eliminate processed foods and grains, you mostly shop the perimeter of the grocery store. That is (mostly) true. But if you look at the pantry staples section, you'll notice that some of those items are not to be found in the perimeter. While there are many places to source our food, I'm going to go through the basics and let you decide which ones fit best into your lifestyle. Remember, this is a zero-judgment zone: Where and how much you spend on food is up to you. For this reason, I trust that you'll purchase the best ingredients available in your area that fit your budget.

GROW YOUR OWN

If I had a dollar for every time someone has suggested that I grow my own food, I'd be rich. Unfortunately for us, this isn't an option. I have a mature rosemary bush in my garden that supplies me with fragrant rosemary for my weekly Rosemary Lemon Chicken (page 97), and that's about it.

Having a small garden is a great option, time and space permitting, if you want to grow in-season vegetables. Depending on where you live and whether you have the time, this might be a fantastic option for you and your family.

FARMERS' MARKETS

Your local farmers' market is a great place to source locally grown fruits and veggies, fresh dairy (if you can have it), grass-fed and hormone-free meats, fresh seafood, wholesome baked goods (usually with gluten- and grain-free options), local honey, plants, seeds, coffee, and more.

Although I don't live near a farmers' market (the closest one is twenty-five minutes away), I know the benefits of having one close by. Getting to know your vendors can provide you with insight on where the food comes from, quality, and possibly the opportunity to order in bulk! Bulk buys = discounts.

CSA BOXES AND GROUP AGRICULTURE PROGRAMS

I've subscribed to a local community-supported agriculture (CSA) program for two out of the last three years. While it gave me the opportunity to try locally grown vegetables every week, the biggest downside was the inability to plan ahead (since you don't always know what you'll be getting) and after five weeks of eating radishes, I ran out of creative ways to cook them.

That said, CSAs can help you save money on farm-fresh produce and allow you to experiment with veggies that might be new to you—if it works for you, it's a great option!

GROCERY STORES

For many of you, this is where much of your weekly fresh produce and staples will be purchased.

Getting rid of processed, grain-based foods may seem a little scary at first—mostly because you can no longer default to boiling spaghetti, adding a little sauce, and calling it dinner—but try to look at it as an opportunity to eat (a lot) more fresh foods. For this reason alone, you'll spend more time in the produce section of your grocery store than ever before.

In winter, when many fruits and vegetables are not in season, I buy a lot of frozen items. Luckily, frozen fruits and vegetables are frozen at their ripest, so their nutritional quality is just as good.

Navigating the grocery aisles can be a bit trickier. You will need to read food labels, often. At the beginning, I kept a running list of my approved brands in my phone (in the notes) so I wouldn't feel the "label overwhelm" coming on. Soon, you will learn which brands work best with your ingredient restrictions and you'll become a label-reading pro!

I purchase many of my weekly staples at the grocery store. They include, but are not limited to, fresh fruit, vegetables, spices, some meats and seafood, deli items, some dairy, small bags of nuts and seeds, and other kitchen necessities.

MEMBERSHIP STORES AND CLUBS

I shop my membership store on a weekly basis for the items that we consume most and also save money by buying in larger quantities (instead of smaller packages from the grocery store).

There, you will find vegetables (onions, celery, carrots, spinach, mushrooms, broccoli, cauliflower, cabbage, salad mix, tomatoes, avocado, etc.), fruits (bananas, strawberries, blueberries, apples, pineapple, mangoes, grapes, oranges, lemons, limes, etc.), frozen fruits and vegetables, nuts and nut butters, seeds, butter, cooking oils (avocado, coconut, olive), wild-caught fish, lean meats, canned tomatoes and olives, canned salmon and tuna, deli meats, eggs, honey, maple syrup, coconut flour, cocoa powder, dairy-free milks, coffee and tea, and many more pantry staples you use daily.

In my experience, it is worth the annual membership fee to belong to one of these stores. I shop there weekly for a lot of my fresh produce and staples for my family of five (and sometimes six with our exchange students). The key to not overspending is to use a shopping list and stick to it!

ONLINE SHOPPING

Easily, the most convenient way to shop for specialty items is online. Websites can deliver difficult-to-find products and, more often than not, at a larger quantity and lower cost.

Some items I purchase regularly online include almond flour, organic coconut milk, coconut aminos, cashews, sunflower seeds, pumpkin seeds, allergy-friendly chocolate chips, tapioca flour, arrowroot starch, and grass-fed gelatin.

Recently, I've discovered several suppliers of grass-fed beef and organic lean meats (chicken, pork, game) online and I've been impressed with the quality, availability, and convenience of overnight shipping straight to my door!

Shopping online can save you a lot of time and money if you're smart about it and take advantage of deals. If you can afford to purchase and store items in bulk, this can be a good option too.

Making Grain-Free Cooking Successful

Grain-free cooking will require a bit more prep work and actual cooking than purchasing freezer meals, cooking out of a box, or ordering takeout, that's for sure. However, there are many things you can do to prepare yourself for success.

If you are new to grain-free cooking, I suggest you follow the recipes in this book as written before revising or adapting them too much. Rome was not built in a day, and neither is learning how to navigate a new cooking style!

The hardest thing about cooking grain-free for my family was making meals appealing enough for my picky eaters. Some recipes will be more successful than others with your family, as was the case with my family, but eventually you'll conquer the kitchen and be able to make one meal for everyone.

For baking recipes, accurate measuring is key and especially crucial in grain-free baking. Unlike roasting veggies, you can't just add "a little extra" for more flavor. When measuring flour, I use the scoop-and-sweep method. Fluff the flour inside your container or package and use a spoon or smaller container to scoop it up and into your measuring cup and then use the back of a knife to sweep the top flat. If you are using a kitchen scale, you'll find all recipes converted to grams for ultimate accuracy.

A final note on substituting ingredients: *coconut flour is not the same as other flours*. This is the question I'm asked most often regarding grain-free cooking and baking. There is no substitute for coconut flour since its unique texture and absorbency are unlike any other flours out there. *Only use coconut flour in recipes that call for it, and don't try using it in recipes that don't.*

Prep-Ahead and Meal Planning

Getting dinner on the table in 30 minutes or less isn't easy to do when you have to make specialty meals for your family. For ultimate mealtime success, it's crucial to plan meals for the week.

Over time, I've found the easiest way to create meal plans is, first, to look at what your week might be like. Will after-school activities keep you away from home later? If so, those meals need to be from the slow cooker section (pages 158 to 169), or quick-and-easy skillet meals (pages 142 to 157).

Making a plan you can follow should take less than a half hour each week. Select your favorite recipes and add a couple of new ones to the rotation. Then, organize them by the amount of time you'll have to prepare the food (no one can start cooking a roast or a slow-cooker soup at 6 p.m.). Once you've selected your recipes, transfer the ingredients you'll need to purchase onto a shopping list. It sounds like a silly reminder but make sure you check your fridge, freezer, and pantry first!

Freezing extra servings or doubling soup recipes such as the All-Meat-and Veggie-Chili (page 162) can also help create freezer meals for another time. Never underestimate the power of your freezer. You can even freeze the Pizza Mini Quiches (page 86) or Spinach and Bacon Mini Quiches (page 89) for quick breakfasts or grab-and-go lunches.

Needless to say, washing produce, marinating meats, prepping the slow cooker early in the morning, or prechopping ingredients are all great ways to save on meal preparation times. I nearly always prep breakfast and make school and office lunches the night before while my kitchen looks like the aftermath of a tornado (from dinner).

Kitchen Tools

Here are a few of the common kitchen tools I find indispensable for meal prep. You certainly don't need to own them all—just pick and choose which ones might work best for you (if you don't own them already).

BLENDER
Grain-free and homemade cooking requires additional preparation. Many high-end blenders can serve as the best smoothie makers, whole-food juicers, and food processors. Some recipes in this book are easy enough to make in any blender. Though, if you don't have a blender that can make batter, use a food processor instead.

FOOD PROCESSOR
This is my second most-used appliance in my kitchen (after my blender). It can chop and grate vegetables and fruit, make nut butters, and purée foods. When selecting a model, I suggest paying a little extra for one with grating attachments; you'll be glad you did.

POTS AND PANS
While I love a new pan, I've found I don't really need that many in my kitchen. The skillet meals in this book assume you are using a large 12-inch (30 cm) pan, or larger. You can also use a wok for those recipes. Family-size recipes that call for a large pot usually refer to a 5.5 or 6-quart (5 to 6 L) pot. Generally, those are the two most important pans in the kitchen. Plus a good small nonstick frying pan is always handy for frying eggs.

SLOW COOKER
This is one handy appliance that will practically cook any meal with minimal effort on busy days. You don't need a very expensive model to cook the recipes in this book; as a matter of fact, most slow cooker recipes in this book were created using the one I received as a wedding gift over a decade ago. In mid-recipe development it finally died and I upgraded to a model with a programmable timer. That is one handy feature I recommend having if you are purchasing a slow cooker for the first time.

SPIRALIZER

This fun and handy tool has become very popular. It yields spiral pasta-like noodles out of vegetables. Since I don't want you to have to purchase a new tool just to make the recipes in this book, I only included four recipes based on my favorite way of eating "zoodles" (spiralized zucchini noodles). If you are thinking of purchasing a spiralizer, check out my video on YouTube/MOMables comparing three popular models.

STAND OR HAND MIXER

Whether you own a large bowl and a handheld mixer or a counter stand mixer, you'll easily be able to use what you have for the couple of recipes in this book that call for this kitchen tool.

LUNCHBOXES AND THERMOSES

Many recipes in this book will yield terrific leftovers that can be warmed up and sent to school or the office inside a thermos!

Generally, a compartmentalized lunchbox and a thermos will be a terrific addition to make the foods in this book portable (especially for grain-free kids' school lunches).

PARCHMENT PAPER

Many recipes in this book call for parchment paper to line a baking pan. You can use a silicone mat instead, although I do recommend keeping a roll of parchment paper handy for rolling out grain-free dough, lining baking pans for easy food removal, and cooking.

OTHER MISCELLANEOUS KITCHEN TOOLS

Knives, chopping block or cutting boards, muffin and mini muffin pans, loaf pans (check the dimensions in the recipe), and baking pans are all tools easily found in any kitchen and called for in this book.

Food Allergies and Substitutions

As mentioned earlier in "What to Expect from This Book" (page 17), the recipes here are much more than just standard grain-free and gluten-free recipes. I designed all the recipes to have lots of flavor while also being able to accommodate a broader food-allergy community.

For your convenience, the recipes have been labeled "dairy-free," "egg-free," and "nut-free," wherever applicable. In addition, I include an "allergy substitution" tip when cutting out an allergen is possible.

Since nut allergies have increased in the last few decades, many schools have a nut-free policy. Make sure you send a note to your child's teacher if you are sending a nut-free butter substitute in your child's lunches or snacks, because alternative nut-free butters look like regular nut butter.

My hope is that this book can help you expand your allergy-friendly recipe repertoire so that you can make one meal that can feed your whole family. That is why I've geared the recipes to be simple enough for anyone to make, with easy-to-find ingredients.

Following, I give you my homemade recipes for Grain-Free Baking Powder (page 32) and my No-Nut Flour (page 32). Most baking powders sold in grocery stores are made with cornstarch. My recipe is a good alternative if you need to avoid corn. The No-Nut Flour is a great nut-free substitute for the baking recipes in this book that call for almond flour or nut flour.

Grain-Free Baking Powder

* DAIRY-FREE   * EGG-FREE   * NUT-FREE

Store-bought baking powder is often made with cornstarch. If you avoid corn, substitute this in a 1:1 ratio wherever store-bought baking powder is used.

1 tablespoon (14 g) baking soda

2 tablespoons (15 g) cream of tartar

2 tablespoons (16 g) tapioca starch

Sift the baking soda, cream of tartar, and tapioca starch into a bowl. Transfer to a glass jar. Seal and store at room temperature up to 1 month.

YIELD: 5 tablespoons (45 g)

No-Nut Flour

* DAIRY-FREE   * EGG-FREE   * NUT-FREE

The flavor of this flour is mildly sweet and nutty, yet neutral enough to use in many baked goods. It's an easy substitute at a 1:1 ratio for almond or nut flour at a fraction of the cost.

1 cup (140 g) raw sunflower seeds or pumpkin seeds

In a food processor, high-speed blender, or coffee grinder, pulse the seeds until they are a flour-like consistency. Avoid overgrinding (in which case you'll have made nut-free butter!) and big chunks by periodically sifting the mixture through a flour sifter or fine-mesh strainer. Repeat grinding the larger pieces until they all pass through the sifting process.

Freeze any leftover No-Nut Flour up to 2 weeks. Avoid making this in large quantities as seed oils tend to go rancid quickly.

YIELD: About ¾ cup (100 g)

- -

KITCHEN NOTE

When using No-Nut Flour in a recipe with baking soda, the baked item may look a little "greenish." This is a result of a chemical reaction between the two ingredients, but it's perfectly safe to eat.

- -

Real Life and Food

The grain-free cooking journey you are about to embark on, or are already living, is hard. It's likely different than anything you've had to do before. It requires more planning and effort in its execution than almost any other eating lifestyle. Try to remember that you are not giving up anything by eliminating grains from your diet—you are gaining health! The truth is that when I removed all grains from my diet, I began to pay attention—even more than before—to the quality of food I was putting into my body.

Remember that your health and the health of your family are worth the fight. We often work really hard on things that aren't related to ourselves (e.g., our jobs, PTA activities, and making other people happy), and forget that we must take care of ourselves first if we truly want to be happy with our lives. Sure, you may temporarily miss macaroni and cheese, cupcakes, breakfast cereal, and donuts, but deep down you know none of those is nutritious or necessary. If you really (really) crave donuts, there are many amazing recipes online that are made with grain-free ingredients—not to mention all the great recipes you'll find in this book.

I still remember the day I felt I'd had enough and needed to make a dietary change. I felt empowered. I wanted to do something so I could feel better. Getting my family to go along with this eating lifestyle, however, has been admittedly a bit more difficult.

There have been many recipes that didn't turn out the way they should, probably due to the learning curve inherent in cooking and baking grain-free recipes (that's the truth) or not being patient enough to read the entire recipe before starting. When the results are less than stellar, the fruits of my hard work are often rejected by my kids and family. Luckily, my husband has jumped on board, since he has experienced firsthand feeling better when following a strict grain-free diet. The most difficult part has been eating outside the home; for this reason, we mostly eat at home or bring food with us to social occasions (more on this later).

I'm often emailed about experiencing resistance to this "new way of eating" by caregivers and family members (e.g., grandparents). My biggest piece of advice is to remember that you are the parent and it is your child's health. Food is medicine and the wrong type of medicine can cause a severe reaction, right? I want you to know you are not alone in this fight for your health!

That said, you can't expect others to jump through hoops to ensure your child's dietary needs are met; it's going to be your job to make sure you pack food for the caregiver or the family member so they don't have to do any extra work.

I've found myself doing a lot of explaining to friends and family about a grain-free lifestyle. In the end, sometimes people just can't understand the science or reasons that anyone would give up whole grains because they are proven to have many benefits. In those cases I remind myself that this is one battle I won't win and that, again, it's my choice to put the right types of foods into my (and my family's) body. Focus on getting the most nutritional bang for your buck in all that you cook, and go from there.

A final note for those of us who are parents and have (in the past) bribed our kids with food. Don't do it. When you live a grain-free lifestyle, you can't say, "do this and you'll get a cupcake" (okay, maybe if you make my Birthday Cupcakes on page 218, but still). Food should not be used as a reward. Instead, reward good behavior with positive experiences; it will greatly help ease the transition into grain-free foods. (For more information on behavior and rewards, check out the MOMables Radio podcasts on iTunes.)

PICKY EATERS

Believe me when I tell you that I have really picky eaters at home. While the recipes I chose for this book are some of my family's favorites, it doesn't mean they are always gobbled up without a fuss. Actually, some of the most difficult recipes to get my kids to try were the ones that eventually became family favorites!

Take it from me—it's a lot easier to stick to the "one meal for everyone" rule than to live resenting the kitchen because it's turned into a restaurant. Provide no alternatives to the meals you've cooked and, yet, always make sure that everyone has one thing in the meal they will eat. I can't tell you how many nights my daughter has traded her meatballs for a heaping bowl of steamed broccoli, while my son doubled up on the meatballs and ate no broccoli. He's just not that into crunchy trees. He will, however, eat it in other forms when the texture is one he likes.

Something that often works well with new meals is to bring everything out to the table and present it family style. This way, kids can choose two of three food items or three out of four of the options you serve. That's mostly my rule—eating "nothing," or mom getting up to make something else are not options.

Stick to your guns and smile! Deliver everything to the table with a huge smile on your face and be confident that they will love it. Kids smell hesitation a mile away and they will often make a fuss at the table to gain attention. I have an entire podcast on MOMables Radio on iTunes where I talk about making mealtime easier. If you need a session filled with even more tips and tricks, that's a fantastic free resource for you.

SOCIAL FUNCTIONS

You've probably realized by now that you are going to have to bring food with you almost everywhere you go. While I suggest that you always let your host know that you or someone in your family has a food sensitivity issue, the truth is that we can't expect everyone to understand how to cook grain-free meals (most people are used to hearing "nut-free" and even "vegetarian" requests since they are much more common). I remember my mother saying, "No grain? Then WHAT CAN YOU EAT?" Everything, it turns out—you just need to be prepared!

When it comes to gatherings, I've come to terms with the fact that it's a lot easier to bring a thermos or a lunchbox of foods that your family can eat than to educate others on how you need to eat. As far as cake and celebrations, I always keep a few baked, frosted, and frozen Birthday Cupcakes (page 218) in my freezer. I'm not afraid of bringing them with me to celebrations so my son can participate.

Dining out at a restaurant is simpler, since you can find salads and a protein-plus-vegetable combination on nearly every menu.

Drive-through and fast food locations are out the window, however, with the exception of a popular Mexican place that offers their burritos in a bowl.

On to the Recipes!

I'm beyond excited to share some of my most precious recipes with you, so let's get to the food, shall we? I hope you experience as much pleasure and joy from these recipes as I did creating them for you!

CHAPTER 2

BREAKFASTS OF CHAMPIONS

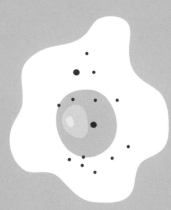

BECAUSE BREAKFAST DOESN'T have to come out of a box! From pancakes and muffins to cereals and scrambles, there's something for everyone.

Silver Dollar Pancakes

* NUT-FREE

I typically make these on a large griddle since I usually have a line of hungry kiddos waiting with their plates in hand.

4 large eggs

1 cup (235 ml) coconut milk

1½ teaspoons pure vanilla extract

1 tablespoon (20 g) honey (optional)

½ cup (65 g) coconut flour

1 teaspoon baking soda

¼ teaspoon salt

Coconut oil, butter, or ghee for cooking

In a blender, combine the eggs, coconut milk, vanilla, and honey until the mixture is thoroughly mixed.

Add the coconut flour, baking soda, and salt and blend. Let the batter sit in the blender for 10 minutes so the coconut flour absorbs the liquid fully.

Grease a pan and set it over medium-high heat. Pour 1½ tablespoons (30 g) of pancake batter into the heated pan. With the back of a spoon, spread out the batter slightly to about 2 inches (5 cm) around. Cook for about 2 minutes on the first side, until golden brown, and flip. Cook the other side for an additional 1 to 2 minutes. Repeat with the remaining batter.

YIELD: 12 small pancakes

- -

KITCHEN NOTE

This recipe works best when the pancakes are kept small.

- -

Blueberry Maple Breakfast Sausage

* NUT-FREE * DAIRY-FREE * EGG-FREE

I first tried this sausage combination from my local store and I've been smitten ever since. Now, it's a regular staple at home.

1 pound (450 g) ground pork

1 garlic clove, minced

2 teaspoons dried sage

¾ teaspoon dried thyme

½ teaspoon dried fennel, crushed

1 teaspoon salt

½ teaspoon freshly ground pepper

3 tablespoons (45 ml) maple syrup

½ cup (75 g) blueberries

1 tablespoon (15 ml) oil, for cooking

In a large mixing bowl, combine the pork, garlic, sage, thyme, fennel, salt, pepper, and maple syrup. Combine mixture thoroughly using your hands. Add blueberries and gently incorporate them to pork mixture.

Form eight 2-inch (5 cm) round patties. Heat a skillet over medium-high heat; cook sausage patties on both sides until cooked through, about 4 minutes per side.

YIELD: 8 sausage patties

- -

KITCHEN NOTE

Double or triple this recipe and freeze for future delicious breakfasts!

- -

Laura's Tip

Make these patties with ground turkey instead of pork for a lighter and just as delicious breakfast sausage.

Blender Bread

*DAIRY-FREE *NUT-FREE OPTION

This grain-free bread is perfect for toasting, grilling, and making sandwiches. It has revolutionized my mornings and lunches!

Oil or butter, for greasing the pan

5 large eggs

2 cups (300 g) cashews

2 tablespoons (28 g) coconut oil, melted

2 tablespoons (16 g) coconut flour

1 teaspoon baking soda

¼ teaspoon salt

1 tablespoon (20 g) honey

1 tablespoon (15 ml) apple cider vinegar

Preheat the oven to 350°F (180°C) and grease a 7 × 3-inch (17.5 × 7.5 cm) pan.

In a high-speed blender, in this order, place the eggs, cashews, coconut oil, coconut flour, baking soda, salt, and honey. Blend until you have a smooth, thick batter. Don't be shy. Blend for 45 seconds to 1 minute.

Add the cider vinegar and blend for about 10 seconds to combine. Immediately transfer to the prepared pan.

Place the pan into the preheated oven on the middle rack. Bake for 45 minutes. After 25 minutes, you may want to cover the loaf lightly with aluminum foil to prevent the top from burning.

Remove from the oven and cool before removing from pan. Refrigerate the bread in an airtight container for up to 5 days.

YIELD: 1 loaf

KITCHEN NOTE

A 7 × 3-inch (17.5 × 7.5 cm) pan in your kitchen arsenal is a must. When this bread is made in a larger loaf pan it will not be as tall and cooking time will need to be adjusted.

Allergy Substitution

Use 2 cups (280 g) of pumpkin or sunflower seeds plus 1 tablespoon (14 g) of coconut oil, butter, or ghee, melted, instead of the cashews. The addition of the coconut oil, butter, or ghee is because the seeds have a lower fat content than the nuts. The loaf will turn a greenish color, as this is what these seeds do when cooked (though the taste won't be compromised).

Cloud Bread

* NUT-FREE

At first glance, it doesn't seem possible that these four ingredients produce bread—incredibly enough, they do! Part roll, part pita, these light, fluffy, spongy creations can be consumed many different ways. My favorite is as hamburger buns. You can also use them for a sandwich or lightly toast and serve with jam. This recipe is not dairy-free, but it's been such a success for so many of my community members I had to include it in this book!

Nonstick cooking spray, for greasing the pans

3 large eggs, carefully separated, making sure no yolk gets in the whites

3 tablespoons (45 g) cream cheese, at room temperature

1 tablespoon (20 g) honey or 2 to 3 drops liquid stevia (optional)

¼ teaspoon cream of tartar

Preheat the oven to 300°F (150°C). Spray two baking sheets well with nonstick cooking spray.

In a small bowl, mix together the egg yolks, cream cheese, and honey (if using) until smooth.

In a larger bowl, combine the egg whites and cream of tartar. Beat the whites on high speed until fluffy and stiff peaks form.

Very carefully fold the egg yolk mixture into the egg whites until thoroughly mixed, being careful not to break down the fluffiness of the egg whites too much.

With a large spoon, scoop the mixture into 10 even rounds on the prepared sheets (roughly ¾-inch [2 cm] thick and 4 to 5 inches [10.2 to 12.7 cm] across).

Place them on the middle rack of the preheated oven and bake for about 30 minutes. Cooking times may vary, so be sure to watch closely and remove them when the tops are golden brown.

Remove from the pans and cool on a rack or cutting board.

Fresh from the oven, these are crumbly and similar to a cooked meringue. Once completely cooled (after being stored overnight in a plastic bag or sealable container), they change in consistency to a softer bread-like texture that is nice and chewy.

YIELD: 10 "clouds"

- -

KITCHEN NOTE
Depending on what you are using these for, you can also add seasonings or spices to taste (cinnamon, nutmeg, garlic powder, etc.). It's a very versatile recipe that can be used for many different purposes!

- -

Strawberry French Toast Muffins

* DAIRY FREE * NUT–FREE OPTION

Quite possibly more convenient to make than traditional French toast (and portable), these muffins are always a winner for a quick breakfast or snack.

2 cups (300 g) cashews

2 large eggs

1 cup (245 g) unsweetened applesauce

2 tablespoons (40 g) honey

2 teaspoons pure vanilla extract

½ teaspoon baking soda

1 teaspoon apple cider vinegar

1 cup (170 g) chopped fresh strawberries

Preheat the oven to 375°F (190°C) and line a 12-cup muffin pan with 10 foil liners.

In a blender or food processor, combine the cashews, eggs, applesauce, honey, vanilla, and baking soda. Blend until the batter is silky smooth and no cashew pieces remain; this may take at least 1 minute. Add the cider vinegar and blend to combine.

Remove the blade and gently fold in the strawberries.

Pour about ¼ cup (120 ml) of batter inside each muffin liner. Place the pan in the preheated oven and bake for 15 minutes, or until the tops are golden brown. Remove from the oven and cool the muffins to room temperature before serving.

YIELD: 10 muffins

- -

KITCHEN NOTE

Foil liners work best for this recipe. If you have paper liners, consider greasing them with a little cooking spray, or generously grease the muffin pan.

- -

Laura's Tip

Turn these muffins into 24 mini muffins. Cooking time will change to about 10 minutes.

Allergy Substitution

Use sunflower seeds or pumpkin seeds instead of cashews for a nut-free version.

Morning Glory Muffins

* DAIRY-FREE * NUT-FREE OPTION

This convenient make-ahead recipe is one I never tire of eating. The muffins will keep well for a few days in the fridge.

½ cup (83 g) ground flaxseed (flax meal)

¼ cup (30 g) walnuts

1 tablespoon (8 g) coconut flour

½ teaspoon ground cinnamon

¼ teaspoon baking soda

¼ teaspoon salt

½ cup (75 g) raisins

3 large eggs

2 tablespoons (28 g) coconut oil, melted

¼ cup (28 g) grated carrot (about 1 large carrot)

Preheat the oven to 350°F (180°C) and line 8 muffin cups with paper liners.

In a food processor, pulse together the flax meal, walnuts, and coconut flour until it resembles coarse sand. Add the cinnamon, baking soda, and salt; pulse a few times to combine.

Add the raisins and pulse again, until they are chopped and incorporated into the mixture (you are not trying to make a paste, just a coarse dough).

Add the eggs and coconut oil and pulse a few times to incorporate. Remove the blade and fold in the carrot just to combine.

Spoon about ¼ cup (125 ml) of batter into the prepared muffin cups. Place them into the preheated oven and bake for 22 minutes, or until a toothpick inserted in the center comes out clean. Cool the muffins for 45 minutes before serving.

YIELD: 8 muffins

Allergy Substitution

Replace the walnuts with ¼ cup (30 g) of sunflower seeds plus 1 additional teaspoon of melted coconut oil.

Blueberry No-Bran Muffins

* DAIRY-FREE * NUT-FREE OPTION

In high school, I went through a bran-muffin-baking craze. Clearly, after you try this no-bran recipe—which is similar, but even better than actual bran muffins—you'll find every excuse to bake them as often as possible. Make the muffin batter ahead of time and refrigerate it overnight. In the morning, bake as directed and enjoy!

½ cup (82 g) ground flaxseed (flax meal)

¼ cup (30 g) walnuts

1 tablespoon (8 g) coconut flour

¼ teaspoon baking soda

¼ teaspoon salt

½ cup (75 g) raisins

3 large eggs

2 tablespoons (28 g) coconut oil, melted

¾ cup (113 g) blueberries

Preheat the oven to 350°F (180°C) and line 6 muffin cups with paper liners.

In a food processor, pulse together the flax meal, walnuts, coconut flour, baking soda, and salt until the mixture resembles sand.

Add the raisins and pulse again, enough to break them down a little.

Pulse in the eggs and coconut oil to combine. For a coarser "bran" muffin texture, pulse for about 10 seconds so the raisins still have some texture; for a smoother texture, purée for 30 seconds.

Remove the blade and carefully fold in the blueberries. You could also pour the batter into a bowl and fold in the blueberries there; I just like to save a few cleanup steps.

Evenly divide the batter among the 6 cups (sometimes a seventh cup if you are liberal with your blueberries).

Place the muffins in the preheated oven and bake for 22 to 25 minutes, or until the tops are firm and a toothpick inserted into the center comes out clean.

Cool the muffins to room temperature before eating.

YIELD: 6 muffins

Allergy Substitution

For a nut-free version, replace the walnuts with ¼ cup (30 g) of sunflower seeds plus 1 additional teaspoon of melted coconut oil.

Peaches and Cream Muffins

* DAIRY-FREE * NUT-FREE

Substitute pineapple or mango chunks for the peaches for a deliciously tropical variation of this recipe.

4 large eggs

1 cup (170 g) chopped fresh peaches or (250 g) frozen, thawed

⅓ cup (80 ml) canned coconut milk

2 tablespoons (40 g) honey

2 tablespoons (28 g) coconut oil, melted

1½ teaspoons pure vanilla extract

½ cup (64 g) coconut flour

½ teaspoon baking soda

¼ teaspoon salt

Preheat the oven to 350°F (180°C). Line a 12-cup muffin pan with 8 paper liners.

In a blender, combine the eggs, peaches, coconut milk, honey, coconut oil, and vanilla until puréed.

Add the coconut flour, baking soda, and salt to the peachy purée. Blend into a thick batter. Allow it to sit in the blender for 10 minutes so the coconut flour absorbs the moisture.

Evenly divide the batter among the 8 paper liners. Place the muffins in the preheated oven and bake for 22 to 25 minutes, or until the tops turn golden brown. Remove from oven and cool the muffins to room temperature before serving.

YIELD: 8 muffins

Pumpkin Chocolate Chip Muffins

* DAIRY-FREE OPTION * NUT-FREE

In the fall, when it's usually on sale, I stock up on canned pumpkin and enjoy these autumn-flavored muffins year-round. They are charmingly fluffy, delicious, and not overly sweet.

1 cup (220 g) pumpkin purée

5 large eggs

1 medium banana, mashed (about ½ cup [113 g])

2 tablespoons (40 g) honey or (30 ml) maple syrup

1 teaspoon pure vanilla extract

2 teaspoons ground cinnamon

1½ teaspoons baking powder

½ cup (64 g) plus 2 tablespoons (16 g) coconut flour

⅓ cup (58 g) nondairy chocolate chips

Preheat the oven to 350°F (180°C) and line a 12-muffin pan with 10 liners.

In a blender, combine the pumpkin purée, eggs, banana, honey, vanilla, and cinnamon.

Once combined, add the baking powder and coconut flour. Mix thoroughly until there are no coconut clumps left. Fold in the chocolate chips and let the mixture sit for 10 minutes so the coconut flour absorbs the liquid.

Fill each muffin liner with about ¼ cup (125 ml) of batter. Place the muffins in the preheated oven and bake for 30 to 33 minutes, or until a toothpick inserted in the center comes out clean.

Remove from the oven and cool the muffins completely. Refrigerate any leftover muffins for up to 4 days.

YIELD: 10 muffins

Blueberry Scones

* DAIRY-FREE * NUT-FREE OPTION

I knew these would be an instant hit at my house when Gabriel, at the age of 18 months, ate two the first time I baked them. To date, they are one of his favorite breakfast treats.

1¾ cups (265 g) almond flour, sifted

3 tablespoons (24 g) coconut flour, sifted

¼ cup (80 g) honey

1 large egg

¼ cup (60 ml) almond milk (any milk will work here), divided

3 tablespoons (42 g) coconut oil or butter, melted

1 teaspoon lemon zest

½ teaspoon baking soda

¼ teaspoon salt

½ cup (75 g) fresh blueberries

Preheat the oven to 350°F (180°C) and line a baking sheet with parchment paper.

To a stand mixer bowl or a large bowl, add the sifted almond flour and coconut flour.

Add the honey, egg, 3 tablespoons (45 ml) of almond milk, coconut oil, lemon zest, baking soda, and salt. Mix until a loose dough forms. Gently fold in the blueberries.

Working on the prepared sheet, fill a biscuit cutter (as your shaper), with about one-sixth of the dough. Press it with your hands to form a scone. Lift the cutter to release it as you hold down the dough. Repeat with the remaining dough.

Brush the scones with the remaining 1 tablespoon (15 ml) of almond milk.

Place the scones into the preheated oven and bake for 18 to 20 minutes, or until golden brown. Cool them slightly before eating.

Store in an airtight container for up to 2 days. Rewarm prior to serving.

YIELD: 6 scones

Laura's Tip

I like to double this recipe and freeze the shaped, unbaked scones on a parchment-lined sheet. Once frozen, I transfer them to a resealable plastic bag and freeze for up to 3 months. To bake, remove them from the freezer while the oven preheats and add 2 to 3 minutes to the baking time.

Allergy Substitution

Substitute No-Nut Flour (page 32) for the almond flour and your milk of choice for the almond milk.

Grain-Free Breakfast Cookies

* DAIRY-FREE * EGG-FREE * NUT-FREE OPTION

Once I completely eliminated grains from my diet and could no longer enjoy the Breakfast Cookie in my book, *The Best Homemade Kids' Lunches on the Planet*, I tirelessly worked on an alternative that would hold its own as the ultimate grain-free breakfast cookie. Serve with fresh fruit for a winning combination.

Cooking spray, for greasing the baking sheets

1 banana

1 cup (260 g) almond butter

⅓ cup (105 g) honey

1 teaspoon pure vanilla extract

½ teaspoon ground cinnamon

1 cup (80 g) finely shredded unsweetened coconut

⅓ cup (47 g) hemp seeds or coarsely chopped sunflower seeds

½ teaspoon baking soda

¼ teaspoon salt

⅓ cup (50 g) raisins (optional)

Preheat the oven to 350°F (180°C). Lightly coat two baking sheets with cooking spray and set aside.

In a large bowl, mash the banana with a fork. Stir in the almond butter, honey, vanilla, and cinnamon.

In a small bowl, combine the coconut, hemp seeds, baking soda, and salt.

Stir the dry ingredients into the banana-almond butter mixture. Fold in the raisins (if using).

Using a ¼-cup (60 ml) measuring cup, drop mounds of dough 3 inches (7.5 cm) apart on the prepared sheets. With a thin metal or small plastic spatula dipped in water, flatten and spread each mound to 2¾ inches (7 cm) round, about ½ inch (1.25 cm) thick.

Bake one sheet at a time, for 14 to 16 minutes, or until browned. Transfer to wire racks to cool completely.

YIELD: 8 cookie-monster-size cookies

KITCHEN NOTE

Refrigerate in an airtight container or resealable plastic bag for up to 4 days or freeze for up to 2 months. Thaw before serving.

Allergy Substitution

Substitute a nut-free butter for the almond butter.

Chocolate Puffs

* EGG-FREE * NUT-FREE OPTION

Just as fun to eat as the ones from the box but with a lot more nutrition and no grains. Get the kids to help roll out the puffs as this is definitely a bit of a labor-intensive recipe.

½ cup (75 g) almond flour

¼ cup (30 g) cocoa powder

½ teaspoon baking powder

¼ teaspoon salt

½ cup (75 g) plus 1 tablespoon (10 g) cashews

2 tablespoons (40 g) honey or (30 ml) maple syrup

1½ tablespoons (25 ml) coconut oil, melted

½ teaspoon pure vanilla extract

Preheat the oven to 375°F (190°C) and line a baking sheet with parchment paper.

Into a food processor, sift the almond flour, cocoa powder, baking powder, and salt.

Add the cashews, honey, coconut oil, and vanilla. Process until thoroughly combined. Just when you think it's done, let it go for 5 minutes more.

Roll the dough into small balls (the size of store-bought chocolate puffs)—preferably with the help of others who will enjoy this treat—and place them on the prepared sheet.

Place the sheet in the preheated oven and bake for 10 minutes. Remove from the oven and cool. Store in an airtight container for up to 1 week.

YIELD: 2 cups (200 g)

- -

KITCHEN NOTE
If you don't have cashews, use walnuts.

- -

Allergy Substitution
Use No-Nut Flour (page 32) instead of the almond flour. Replace the cashews with either sunflower seeds or pumpkin seeds.

Fruit-at-the-Bottom Yogurt

* DAIRY-FREE * EGG-FREE * NUT-FREE OPTION

Making your own yogurt is super easy and budget friendly. Why pay the hefty prices for the dairy-free alternatives at the store?

2 tablespoons (30 ml) warm water

1½ teaspoons powdered gelatin

2 cups (475 ml) unsweetened vanilla almond milk

2 tablespoons (30 ml) maple syrup or (40 g) honey

¾ cup (240 g) Easy Fruit Jam (page 59)

In a small bowl, stir together the warm water and gelatin and let it sit for 10 minutes to form a jelly-like mixture.

Meanwhile, in a medium saucepan set over low heat, whisk together the almond milk and maple syrup. Warm the milk until hot, just before boiling, stirring often. Remove from the heat and allow to cool down to 120°F (48°C).

Whisk ¼ cup (60 ml) of warm milk into the gelatin mixture until it completely dissolves. Pour the gelatin mixture back into the saucepan and whisk to combine.

Place 1½ tablespoons (30 g) of jam in the bottom of each of four 6-ounce (175-ml) glass yogurt ramekins or Mason jars. Fill each with the milk mixture, leaving about ½ inch (1.25 cm) of room on top. Cool to room temperature, cover, and refrigerate overnight.

YIELD: 4 servings

KITCHEN NOTE

For thicker—and more nutritious—yogurt, use 1 cup (235 ml) canned coconut milk and 1 cup (235 ml) almond milk (instead of 2 cups [470 ml] almond milk).

Laura's Tip

Add probiotics to this yogurt by mixing one 25 to 50 billion CFUs probiotic pill into the gelatin. First, wait until the milk has cooled to room temperature before combining the gelatin mixture with the milk.

Allergy Substitution

Use a nut-free milk instead of the almond milk.

Breakfast Apple Pie

* DAIRY–FREE OPTION   * EGG–FREE   * NUT–FREE OPTION

Few things are better than waking up to the smell of freshly baked apple pie. This breakfast option delivers just that and keeps your gut healthy.

Oil or butter, for greasing the pan

3 or 4 large apples, washed, cored, unpeeled, and cut into small chunks

2 tablespoons (30 ml) fresh lemon juice (about 1 lemon)

1 teaspoon ground cinnamon, divided

1 cup (150 g) almond flour

¼ cup (30 g) walnuts, chopped

¼ cup (55 g) butter or coconut oil, melted

2 tablespoons (30 ml) maple syrup or (40 g) honey

Preheat the oven to 375°F (190°C) and grease a 9 × 9-inch (23 × 23 cm) baking dish.

In a large bowl, toss together the apples, lemon juice, and ¾ teaspoon of cinnamon until the apples are evenly coated. Transfer to the prepared dish.

In a medium bowl, combine the almond flour, walnuts, butter, maple syrup, and remaining ¼ teaspoon of cinnamon.

Spread the nut topping evenly over the apples. Place the dish in the preheated oven and bake for 40 to 45 minutes, or until the apples are soft and bubbly on the sides.

YIELD: 6 servings

Laura's Tip

Make this easy dish even easier. Prep this delicious warm breakfast the night before. In the morning, all you have to do is bake and enjoy!

Allergy Substitution

Substitute No-Nut Flour (see page 32) for the almond flour. Omit the walnuts or use ¼ cup (20 g) of shredded unsweetened coconut instead.

Cream-of Cereal

* DIARY-FREE * EGG-FREE
* NUT-FREE OPTION

I love a hearty bowl of this warm "cereal" in the morning. It packs a lot more fiber and nutrition than the one found in a box.

1½ cups (354 ml) unsweetened almond milk

½ cup (113 g) ripe mashed banana (about 1 medium banana)

⅓ cup (43 g) coconut flour

¼ cup (20 g) unsweetened shredded coconut

½ teaspoon cinnamon

1 tablespoon (20 g) honey or (15 ml) maple syrup (optional)

In a blender, combine the almond milk, banana, coconut flour, coconut, and cinnamon. Blend until the mixture is thick and combined. Transfer to a small pot.

Place the pot over high heat and bring to a boil, making sure you stir it often. Reduce the heat to low, cover, and simmer for 2 minutes. Stir a couple of times throughout. Turn off the heat and let the mixture sit for about 5 minutes. Alternately, the "cereal" can be warmed in a microwave-safe dish in the microwave.

Remove from the heat, divide between 2 bowls, and drizzle with honey or maple syrup (if using).

YIELD: 2 servings

Allergy Substitution

Use any nut-free milk instead of the almond milk.

Nutty No-Oat Meal

* DAIRY-FREE * EGG-FREE
* NUT-FREE OPTION

During a business trip, I ordered a version of this morning cereal for a week straight from room service. I came home determined to make my own. It gives everyone a nutritious, filling start to their day. Double or triple the recipe and keep it refrigerated for up to 1 week. In the morning, give the mixture a quick stir before heating.

½ cup (75 g) cashews

½ cup (60 g) walnuts

1 tablespoon (10 g) chia seeds

1½ teaspoons whole flaxseed or 1 tablespoon (8 g) ground flaxseed (flax meal)

1¼ cups (300 ml) unsweetened almond milk

2 tablespoons (18 g) raisins

¾ teaspoon ground cinnamon

In a blender, combine the cashews, walnuts, chia seeds, flaxseed, almond milk, raisins, and cinnamon. Blend until the mixture is smooth but some nutty chunks remain. Let it sit inside the blender for 5 minutes to thicken.

Warm the cereal in the microwave or on the stovetop before serving.

YIELD: 2 servings

Allergy Substitution

For a nut-free version, substitute sunflower seeds or pumpkin seeds for the walnuts and cashews, and use your favorite nut-free milk alternative for the almond milk.

Sweet Potato Morning Scramble

* NUT-FREE

This delicious, lightly spiced scramble is often enjoyed on Sunday mornings at my house. It's so good I often make it on our breakfast-for-dinner night, too.

8 large eggs

⅓ cup (80 ml) milk of choice

½ teaspoon ground cumin

¼ teaspoon salt

¼ teaspoon freshly ground black pepper

1 tablespoon (14 g) butter

1 pound (450 g) sweet potatoes (2 medium), peeled, quartered lengthwise, and thinly sliced

1 scallion, finely chopped, plus more for garnish

2 cups (60 g) fresh baby spinach

Fresh parsley, chopped (optional)

In a medium bowl, whisk together the eggs, milk, cumin, salt, and pepper. Set aside.

In a large skillet set over medium heat, melt the butter. Add the sweet potatoes and scallion. Cook for about 8 minutes, or just until the potatoes are tender and lightly browned, stirring occasionally.

Add the spinach and cook for about 1 minute, stirring until wilted.

Pour the egg mixture into the skillet over the sweet potato mixture. Cook over medium heat, without stirring, until the eggs begin to set on the bottom and around the edges. They'll be floppy, but no longer runny. Using a spatula or large spoon, lift and fold the partially cooked eggs so the uncooked eggs are near the heat and cook through.

Once cooked, remove from the heat, and sprinkle with the additional scallions and parsley (if using).

YIELD: 4 to 6 servings

Easy Fruit Jam

* DAIRY-FREE * EGG-FREE * NUT-FREE

This recipe works well with berries, peaches, pineapple, mango, apples, pears, and most moderate-water-dense fruits.

2 cups (155 g) chopped fresh fruit of choice or frozen, thawed

2 tablespoons (20 g) chia seeds

½ teaspoon pure vanilla extract

In a medium pot set over medium-high heat, bring the fruit to a boil, stirring often. Reduce the heat to low and simmer until the fruit begins to soften and release its juices.

Using a potato masher or the back of a ladle, mash the fruit to a thick purée, leaving a few chunks for texture. Stir in the chia seeds, reduce the heat to low, and continue cooking for 5 minutes more, stirring often.

Once the fruit has a jam-like texture, remove it from the heat and stir in the vanilla.

Cool the jam to room temperature before transferring it to a glass container.

Keep refrigerated for up to 2 weeks.

YIELD: About 1½ cups (480 g)

Laura's Tip

Freeze the jam in 1-cup (320 ml) quantities in freezer bags to be enjoyed year-round.

Drop Biscuits

* DAIRY-FREE OPTION * EGG-FREE * NUT-FREE OPTION

Crispy on the outside and fluffy and delicious inside, these drop biscuits are my family's favorite for breakfast or as a delicious alternative to dinner rolls.

½ cup (120 ml) plus 1 tablespoon (15 ml) coconut milk

½ teaspoon apple cider vinegar

2 cups (300 g) almond flour

½ cup (65 g) tapioca starch

½ teaspoon salt

½ teaspoon baking soda

1 tablespoon (14 g) baking powder

5 tablespoons (70 g) butter, grated

Preheat the oven to 350°F (180°C) and line a baking sheet with parchment paper.

In a measuring cup or small bowl, combine the coconut milk and cider vinegar and set aside.

In a large bowl or the bowl of your food processor, combine the almond flour, tapioca starch, salt, baking soda, and baking powder.

Cut or pulse the butter into the dry ingredients until it resembles pebbly, coarse sand. Add the coconut milk mixture and combine.

Drop ¼-cup (45 g) scoops of dough onto the prepared sheet. Place the sheet in the preheated oven and bake for 15 minutes, or until lightly golden brown.

YIELD: 10 biscuits

- -

KITCHEN NOTE

Butter is easiest to grate when it's very cold or frozen.

- -

Allergy Substitution

Use No-Nut Flour (page 32) instead of almond flour. Substitute refrigerated ghee for the butter.

Shakshuka

*DAIRY-FREE *NUT-FREE

Don't let the fancy look (or name) of this traditional Middle Eastern breakfast dish fool you. It's easier than it looks. The tomato and veggies make a delicious and nutritious base for the protein-rich filling. I've taken the classic recipe and toned down the seasoning to give the recipe ultimate kid appeal.

1 tablespoon (15 ml) olive oil

½ cup (80 g) finely chopped onion

1 red bell pepper, chopped

1 garlic clove, minced

1 teaspoon mild chili powder

1 teaspoon ground cumin

1 teaspoon paprika

½ teaspoon coconut palm sugar (optional)

½ teaspoon salt

¼ teaspoon freshly ground black pepper

2 cans (14.5 ounces, or 410 g) petite diced tomatoes

6 large eggs

Fresh parsley (optional)

Preheat the oven to 375°F (190°C).

In a large ovenproof skillet set over medium heat, heat the olive oil. Add the onion and red bell pepper. Cook for 7 to 8 minutes, stirring frequently, or until the onion is translucent and the red bell pepper softens.

Add the garlic, chili powder, cumin, paprika, coconut palm sugar, salt, and pepper to the pan. Cook for 1 minute more to toast the spices.

Add the tomatoes and stir to combine. Reduce the heat to medium-low and cook the mixture for about 10 minutes.

Crack the eggs on top of the tomato mixture, making sure you distribute the eggs evenly around the skillet. Transfer the skillet to the preheated oven and bake for about 8 minutes, or until the eggs are set.

Remove from the oven and sprinkle with parsley (if using).

YIELD: 4 to 6 servings

Nut Clusters

* DAIRY-FREE * EGG-FREE * NUT-FREE OPTION

Crunchy, delicious, and just like the clusters found inside the cereal but without the grains.

4 cups (525 g) mixed nuts (pecans, almonds, walnuts) or 4 cups (460 g) seeds, half sunflower and half pumpkin

1¾ teaspoons salt, divided

Water, as needed

2 tablespoons (28 g) coconut oil, melted

1 tablespoon (7 g) ground cinnamon

½ cup (160 g) honey or (120 ml) pure maple syrup, melted

2 tablespoons (30 ml) pure vanilla extract

¼ cup (41 g) ground flaxseed (flax meal)

Optional add-ins (up to 1 cup [150 g] total combined):

½ cup (43 g) unsweetened shredded coconut

½ cup (75 g) raisins

½ cup (60 g) dried blueberries

½ cup (60 g) dried cranberries

The day before baking: In a large bowl, combine the mixed nuts or seeds, and 1 teaspoon of salt. Cover completely with water and set aside. Soak for 12 hours (overnight) at room temperature, changing the water once before baking, about halfway through.

The day of baking: In a colander, drain the nuts or seeds and give them a rinse. Place them on a few layers of paper towels or a clean kitchen towel to absorb any remaining water.

Preheat the oven to 200°F (93°C). Line 2 baking trays with parchment paper or silicone mats and set aside.

In a food processor, pulse the nuts or seeds a few times to chop them into small pieces. (If you turn on your food processor and let it go, you'll have flour, instead).

In a large bowl, stir together the coconut oil, cinnamon, honey, vanilla, and remaining ¾ teaspoon of salt. Add the finely chopped nuts or seeds and the flaxseed to the bowl. With a spatula, mix well until everything is covered in cinnamon-vanilla goodness. Stir in the coconut (if using).

Spread the mix onto the prepared sheets and place them in the preheated oven for about 3 hours. Swap racks and turn the trays every hour, moving the mixture around to get it evenly dehydrated. After 3 hours, remove the trays from the oven. Check the crunch level. The mixture needs to be fully dehydrated. Either return to the oven for another 30 minutes or remove and let cool. They will crunch as they cool.

Note: If you use only 1 tray, expect dehydrating time to take 45 minutes to 1 hour longer.

If you want to add dried fruit, this is the time. Stir in the dried fruit of choice, then cool the mixture completely before storing in an airtight container for 2 to 3 weeks.

YIELD: 4 to 5 cups (460 to 656 g)

- -

KITCHEN NOTE

Any nut combination will work, but make sure you use between 3½ to 4 cups (420 to 480 g) total.

- -

CHAPTER 3
LUNCHBOX FAVORITES

BECAUSE GRAIN-FREE LUNCHES can get
repetitive, I've included some of my favorite recipes
in this section to give you alternatives and
prevent boredom. They are perfect for school,
office lunches, and anytime you need food to go!

Crunchy Tuna Salad Cups

* DAIRY-FREE * NUT-FREE

High in protein and with omega-3s, these cups make this healthy tuna salad a lot more fun to eat for everyone in the family!

2 cans (6 ounces, or 340 g) tuna, drained

1 cup (100 g) finely chopped celery

1 medium carrot, finely shredded

2 tablespoons (12 g) sliced scallions

½ teaspoon dried dill

¼ teaspoon garlic powder

⅓ cup (75 g) mayonnaise or Homemade Mayonnaise (page 68)

Juice of 1 lemon

1 teaspoon lemon zest

8 green or butter lettuce leaves, washed

In a medium bowl, stir together the tuna, celery, carrot, scallions, dill, garlic powder, mayonnaise, lemon juice, and lemon zest.

Evenly divide the tuna salad among the 8 lettuce leaves and serve.

YIELD: 4 servings

Homemade Salsa ▷

* DAIRY-FREE * EGG-FREE * NUT-FREE

Looking for an easy salsa recipe that tastes just as good as those you enjoy in restaurants? Look no further. This recipe is super easy, and kids will love it, too, since it has just the right amount of spice. Try it with Plantain Chips (page 214). Dip in and enjoy!

1 can (14.5 ounces, or 410 g) fire-roasted tomatoes, with juices

1 can (14.5 ounces, or 410 g) petite diced tomatoes, with juices

1 small onion, roughly chopped

1 or 2 jalapeño peppers, stemmed and seeded

3 garlic cloves, peeled

1½ teaspoons ground cumin

1 teaspoon salt

Juice of 1 lime

⅓ cup (5 g) chopped fresh cilantro

To a blender or food processor, add the fire-roasted tomatoes, diced tomatoes, onion, jalapeños, garlic, cumin, salt, lime juice, and cilantro, in the order listed. Pulse to combine and then blend on medium speed, gradually increasing to high speed until the texture is nearly smooth.

Refrigerate for 1 hour before serving. Keep leftovers refrigerated for up to 1 week.

YIELD: 4 cups (950 ml)

Pineapple–Avocado Salad

*DAIRY-FREE *EGG-FREE *NUT-FREE

This creamy, tropical salad will make you feel like you are having a poolside lunch on vacation.

2 cups (330 g) fresh pineapple chunks, diced small

1 pint (300 g) cherry tomatoes, quartered

½ cup (80 g) finely chopped red onion

¼ cup (32 g) roasted salted sunflower seeds

½ jalapeño pepper, finely chopped

¼ cup (60 ml) avocado oil or olive oil

Juice of 1 lemon (about 2 tablespoons [30 ml])

Salt and freshly ground black pepper, to taste

3 avocados, peeled, pitted, and sliced

In a large bowl, combine the pineapple, tomatoes, red onion, sunflower seeds, jalapeño, avocado oil, and lemon juice. Season with salt and pepper. Toss the mixture to combine thoroughly.

Add the avocado and give the salad a quick toss to incorporate it throughout.

YIELD: 4 servings

Homemade Mayonnaise

*DAIRY-FREE *NUT-FREE

I grew up watching my grandmother make mayonnaise. I didn't know there was such a thing as store-bought mayonnaise until I came to the United States in my teens. To date, I use her method and age-old basic recipe.

1 large egg yolk

1 teaspoon fresh lemon juice

1 teaspoon white wine vinegar

½ teaspoon salt

¼ teaspoon Dijon mustard

¾ cup (175 ml) avocado oil or olive oil

In a blender, combine the egg yolk, lemon juice, white wine vinegar, salt, and Dijon mustard. Blend until combined.

With the blender on medium-low, slowly drizzle in the oil until the mixture resembles mayonnaise and all of the oil is incorporated.

Cover and refrigerate for 1 hour. Leftovers can be refrigerated in an airtight container for up to 5 days.

YIELD: ¾ cup (175 g)

Salmon Salad

* DAIRY–FREE * NUT–FREE

This nutrient-rich salad is also filled with protein and healthy omega-3s.

1 can (7 ounces, or 209 g) salmon, drained

1½ tablespoons (21 g) Homemade Mayonnaise (page 68)

¼ cup (25 g) finely chopped celery

Juice of ½ of a lemon

⅛ teaspoon freshly ground black pepper

In a large bowl, crumble and separate the salmon, checking for possible bones. Add the mayonnaise, celery, lemon juice, and pepper. Gently fold to combine all ingredients.

YIELD: 2 servings

Avocado Egg Salad

* NUT–FREE

This is my go-to high-protein lunch recipe because it's filled with healthy fats and provides incredible nutritional value.

2 avocados, peeled and pitted

4 large hardboiled eggs

2 tablespoons (28 g) Homemade Mayonnaise (page 68), plus additional as needed

1 tablespoon (15 ml) fresh lime juice (about ½ of a lime)

¼ teaspoon salt

In a food processor, pulse together the avocado flesh, eggs, mayonnaise, lime juice, and salt to your desired consistency. Some egg pieces should be noticeable. For a smoother consistency, add additional mayonnaise.

Keep refrigerated for up to 3 days.

YIELD: 4 servings

Easy Guacamole

* DAIRY-FREE * EGG-FREE * NUT-FREE

When my avocados get too ripe to eat, I make guacamole with this easy recipe. Not only is it a delicious party in a bowl, but the healthy fats, such as the ones found in avocados, are great for the cardiovascular system, hair, skin, and your overall health. They are also rich in fiber, potassium, vitamin K, copper, folate, and B vitamins.

3 ripe avocados, pitted

½ to ¾ cup (130 to 195 g) fresh salsa, liquid drained or Homemade Salsa (page 66)

In a bowl, scoop out the avocado flesh and mash it with a fork, making some of the texture smooth and leaving a few chunky pieces. Mix in the salsa and serve.

YIELD: 4 to 6 servings

Tuna Avocado Salad

* DAIRY-FREE * EGG-FREE * NUT-FREE

This tuna avocado salad is one of my go-to recipes for a healthy dose of fats, omega-3s, and protein. It's perfect on top of a bed of spinach or as filler for lettuce cups. Once in a while, when I am feeling the need for a sandwich, I spread this delicious salad between two slices of grain-free Blender Bread (page 40).

2 avocados, peeled, pitted, and mashed

2 cans (6 ounces, or 170 g) tuna, drained

1 teaspoon all-purpose seasoning of choice

In a large bowl, combine the avocados, tuna, and seasoning. Mix together with a fork and serve.

YIELD: 4 servings

Arriba! Seasoning

* DAIRY-FREE * EGG-FREE * NUT-FREE

This is very similar to taco seasoning, but with a smoky flavor, less spice, and a whole lot of kid appeal.

3 tablespoons (22.5 g) chili powder

2 tablespoons (14 g) ground cumin

1 tablespoon (7 g) paprika

2 teaspoons black pepper

2 teaspoons garlic powder

2 teaspoons dried oregano

1½ teaspoons salt

1 teaspoon onion powder

In a small bowl, stir together the chili powder, cumin, paprika, pepper, garlic powder, oregano, salt, and onion powder. Store in an airtight container.

YIELD: 9 tablespoons (69 g)

Egg Salad

DAIRY-FREE *NUT-FREE*

The variations of egg salad recipes are endless and, yet, this is my family's favorite.

4 large hard-boiled eggs, peeled and diced

1 tablespoon (11 g) Dijon mustard

1 teaspoon paprika

1 tablespoon (3 g) chopped chives (optional)

2 tablespoons (28 g) Homemade Mayonnaise (page 68)

In a large bowl, combine the eggs, mustard, paprika, chives (if using), and mayonnaise. Stir to combine thoroughly. Cover and refrigerate.

YIELD: 2 servings

Laura's Tip

This salad comes together quickly when you have perfectly hardboiled eggs in the fridge.

How to Hard-Boil Perfect Eggs

Watch these being made on YouTube/MOMables. Note: You need to cover the eggs fully with at least 2 inches (5 cm) of water for this cooking method to work. Less water means it cools quicker and your eggs won't cook thoroughly.

Large eggs, any quantity

Cold water

1 tablespoon (18 g) salt

In a medium saucepan, fully cover the eggs with at least 2 inches (5 cm) of cold water. Add the salt.

Place the pan over high heat until it reaches a boil. Turn off the heat, cover, and let sit for 13 minutes.

After exactly 13 minutes, drain the eggs and place them back in the pot. Fill the pot with cold water and ice, until the eggs are covered. Cool the eggs for 5 minutes.

Remove the eggs from the cold water and carefully crack the eggshells, making sure the majority of the shell is cracked. Gently begin removing the shells, dipping the egg back into the cold water to help separate the egg from the membrane. The ice-water bath will "shock" the membrane between the egg white and the shell, loosening the shell and allowing you to peel it off in nearly one piece.

Serve immediately, use in a recipe, make egg salad, or keep refrigerated for 3 days.

- -

KITCHEN NOTE

The salt won't affect the flavor of your eggs; it helps solidify the proteins within the egg, helping create an easier-to-peel egg!

- -

Honey Mustard Vinaigrette

* DAIRY-FREE * EGG-FREE * NUT-FREE

This is my go-to dressing for big bowls of crispy greens and leftover grilled chicken. Simple, fresh, and delicious!

1 garlic clove, minced

1 tablespoon (15 ml) white wine vinegar

1½ teaspoons Dijon mustard

1 teaspoon honey

⅛ teaspoon salt

Freshly ground black pepper, to taste

⅓ cup (80 ml) extra-virgin olive oil

In a small bowl, whisk together the garlic, vinegar, mustard, honey, salt, and pepper. Slowly whisk in the olive oil until the dressing is thoroughly combined.

Refrigerate leftovers for up to 1 week.

YIELD: ½ cup (120 ml)

Everyday Herb Vinaigrette

* DAIRY-FREE * EGG-FREE * NUT-FREE

This is an everyday dressing that goes well with practically everything. From salads to marinating chicken this is a great staple to keep in your fridge.

⅓ cup (80 ml) extra-virgin olive oil

⅓ cup (80 ml) white wine vinegar

2 tablespoons (5 g) chopped fresh herbs (thyme, oregano, basil) or ¼ cup (8 g) dried herbs

1 teaspoon Dijon mustard

1 garlic clove, grated

¼ teaspoon salt

⅛ teaspoon freshly ground black pepper

In a dressing bottle or screw-top jar, combine the olive oil, white wine vinegar, herbs, mustard, garlic, salt, and pepper. Cover and shake well to combine.

Serve immediately or keep refrigerated, covered, for up to 4 days if using fresh herbs or 1 week if using dried herbs.

YIELD: ¾ cup (175 ml)

Laura's Tip

This is the perfect dressing to make to use up any leftover fresh herbs from your meal prep.

Raspberry Vinaigrette

* DAIRY-FREE * EGG-FREE * NUT-FREE

Fruity and fresh, this is one salad dressing worth eating daily.

½ cup (65 g) fresh raspberries

2 teaspoons honey

⅓ cup (80 ml) white balsamic vinegar

⅓ cup (80 ml) extra-virgin olive oil

¼ teaspoon salt

⅛ teaspoon freshly ground black pepper

In a medium bowl, mash the raspberries with a fork and transfer to a lidded dressing bottle or screw-top jar.

Add the honey, vinegar, olive oil, salt, and pepper. Cover and shake well to combine.

Serve immediately or refrigerate, covered, for up to 3 days.

YIELD: About ¾ cup (175 ml)

Laura's Tip

Use a blender for a smooth texture.

Veggie Cups with Homemade Ranch Dressing ▶

* DAIRY-FREE OPTION * NUT-FREE

Having these premade and ready to go to toss inside a lunchbox or as a handy snack makes my life good! The ranch dressing is multipurpose. Use it as a salad dressing and a dip! It will become a favorite.

For the Homemade Ranch Dressing:

½ cup (115 g) Homemade Mayonnaise (page 68)

½ cup (120 ml) buttermilk or coconut milk

1 teaspoon garlic powder

1 teaspoon dill weed

½ teaspoon onion powder

¼ teaspoon salt

Freshly ground black pepper, to taste

For serving:

8 cups (850 g) chopped mixed veggies (carrots, celery, peppers, etc.)

To make the Homemade Ranch Dressing: In a medium bowl, whisk together the mayonnaise, buttermilk, garlic powder, dill, onion powder, and salt. Season with pepper.

You will need ½ cup (120 ml) of dressing for the veggie cups. Refrigerate the remaining ½ cup (120 ml) in an airtight container for up to 4 days.

To serve: Wash and chop the veggies on a cutting board, making sure the veggie pieces are slightly smaller than the serving/storage cups.

Place about 1 tablespoon (15 ml) of ranch dressing at the bottom of each cup. Fill each container with about 1 cup (106 g) of vertically placed veggies.

YIELD: 8 cups (850 g) veggies, plus 1 cup (235 ml) dressing

Seven-Layer Greek Cups

*EGG-FREE *NUT-FREE

Need a fun and healthy school lunch idea? One that will get you and "A+" and help get an extra serving of veggies in the kids? If so, you are going to love these!

1 container (10 ounces, or 285 g) hummus, divided

¼ cup (38 g) crumbled feta cheese

½ cup (50 g) pitted kalamata olives, drained and chopped

2 tablespoons (12 g) chopped roasted or fresh red bell peppers

1 small tomato, diced

1 small cucumber, diced

1 tablespoon (4 g) chopped fresh oregano

Plantain Chips (page 214), for serving

In each of 4 individual 8-ounce (235 ml) lidded containers, spread about 2 tablespoons (30 g) of hummus along the bottom.

Sprinkle the hummus with equal amounts of the feta, olives, red bell peppers, tomato, and cucumber.

Garnish with oregano and serve with the plantain chips. Refrigerate for up to 3 days.

YIELD: 4 individual cups

Fennel and Orange Salad

*DAIRY-FREE *EGG-FREE *NUT-FREE

My mom often makes this salad when I come over for lunch. We mix it all in a big bowl and feast on its freshness.

1 large or 2 small fresh fennel bulbs

2 small oranges or 1 large orange

2 tablespoons (30 ml) olive oil

Salt and freshly ground black pepper, to taste

1 tablespoon (15 ml) fresh lemon juice or fresh orange juice

¼ cup (15 g) chopped Italian flat-leaf parsley

Cut the fennel bulbs in half lengthwise and then trim the bottom from each half. Thinly slice the fennel halves horizontally, for crescent-shaped slices near the bottom, and as high up as you can before you get to the fronds. You can also use a mandoline for this. Place the slices on the serving dish.

Peel and slice the orange with a sharp knife. Start by cutting off the top and bottom of the orange. Then, work around it, slicing off the peel in horizontal strips until the orange is bare. Cut the orange in half horizontally, and then break it down into thick wedges. Put the orange slices on top of the fennel.

Drizzle the olive oil over the top. Season with salt and pepper, and then sprinkle a little lemon juice on top.

Top with the parsley and serve.

YIELD: 4 side servings

Veggie Falafels

* DAIRY-FREE   * NUT-FREE OPTION

When I'm out of chickpeas or following a strict Paleo diet with no legumes, this is my go-to recipe for falafel. Eat them alone or top a colorful salad and you've got yourself a healthy and satisfying meal!

1 cup (160 g) roughly chopped onion

½ cup (8 g) fresh cilantro

½ cup (30 g) fresh parsley

4 garlic cloves

2 cups (200 g) cauliflower florets

1 zucchini, roughly chopped

Zest of 1 lemon

2 teaspoons ground cumin

½ teaspoon turmeric

¼ teaspoon chili powder

½ cup (48 g) almond flour

1 large egg, beaten

Salt and freshly ground black pepper, to taste

Melted coconut oil, for greasing the pan and coating the falafels

Preheat the oven to 375°F (190°C).

In a food processor, pulse together the onion, cilantro, parsley, and garlic until finely minced. Transfer to a large bowl and set aside.

Repeat the process with the cauliflower and the zucchini; add to the bowl with the onion mixture.

Add the lemon zest, cumin, turmeric, chili powder, almond flour, and beaten egg to the vegetables. Stir to combine well. Season with salt and pepper. Let the mixture rest for a few minutes.

Spread some melted coconut oil over a baking sheet. With clean hands, form medium-size balls of the falafel mixture and place them on the prepared sheet. Brush more oil over the falafels and place them in the preheated oven. Bake for 40 minutes, turning halfway through and brushing with more oil.

Alternately, you can cook the falafels on the stovetop. In a large sauté pan placed over medium heat, heat a generous amount of coconut oil for about 4 minutes. Then, add the falafel, browning them on one side for 4 minutes, flipping once, and browning the other side for about 3 minutes more, or until golden and cooked through.

YIELD: 4 to 6 servings

Allergy Substitution

Substitute No-Nut Flour (page 32) for the almond flour.

Cobb Salad Cups

* *DAIRY-FREE* * *NUT-FREE*

Perfectly portable to the office or school, these Cobb Salad Cups are filled with all the crunch of fresh veggies and they fill you with great taste and nutrients galore.

1 head of iceberg lettuce, washed

1 pint (298 g) cherry tomatoes

2 avocados, peeled, pitted, and diced

2 large hard-boiled eggs, peeled and diced

8 ounces (225 g) deli turkey, chopped

½ cup (80 g) chopped red onion

¼ cup (60 ml) of your favorite dressing (or one from pages 73 to 74)

On each of 4 plates, layer 2 to 3 lettuce leaves to form a sturdy base for the salad.

Evenly divide the tomatoes, avocado, eggs, turkey, and red onion among the lettuce cups. Drizzle with the dressing and serve.

YIELD: 4 servings

Seven-Layer Mexican Cups ▷

* *EGG-FREE* * *NUT-FREE*

I love single-serve versions of party favorites. These lunch cups are filling, full of protein and fiber, and a lot of fun to eat!

1 can (15 ounces, or 425 g) black beans, rinsed and drained

1 package (8 ounces, or 225 g) guacamole or 1 cup (225 g) Easy Guacamole (page 71)

1 cup (230 g) sour cream

1 cup (260 g) fresh salsa or Homemade Salsa (page 66)

1 cup (115 g) shredded sharp Cheddar cheese

2 medium tomatoes, finely diced

8 ounces (170 g) sliced black olives

Minced scallion, for topping

On your work surface, line up all the ingredients and 6 small lidded jars or plastic cups.

Layer each cup with about 2 tablespoons of each ingredient: black beans, guacamole, sour cream, salsa, Cheddar cheese, tomatoes, and black olives. Top with the scallion and refrigerate.

YIELD: 6 to 8 dip cups

Peanut and Chicken Lettuce Cups

* DAIRY-FREE * EGG-FREE * NUT-FREE OPTION

Full of flavor and easy to make, these cups are inevitably the type of dish you'd order repeatedly at your favorite lunch spot.

2 tablespoons (30 ml) oil

1 pound (454 g) boneless skinless chicken breast halves, cut into 1-inch (2.5 cm) pieces

¼ cup (80 g) peanuts, chopped

3 garlic cloves, minced

2 teaspoons minced fresh ginger

¼ cup (25 g) sliced scallions

1 tablespoon (15 ml) coconut aminos

2 teaspoons apple cider vinegar

1 teaspoon toasted sesame oil

8 green lettuce or butter lettuce leaves, washed

Lime wedges (optional)

In a large skillet set over medium-high heat, warm the oil. Add the chicken and cook for 2 to 3 minutes, or until it is no longer pink.

Add the peanuts, garlic, and ginger. Continue cooking for another 3 minutes, or until the chicken is browned on all sides.

Add the scallions, coconut aminos, cider vinegar, and sesame oil to the skillet. Continue cooking until the chicken is thoroughly cooked and the liquid has simmered for about 1 minute.

Evenly divide the chicken mixture among the 8 lettuce leaves. Sprinkle with cilantro, and squeeze a lime wedge or two (if using) over the chicken.

YIELD: 4 servings

Allergy Substitution

Replace the peanuts with ¼ cup (16 g) of chopped pumpkin seeds or (36 g) sunflower seeds.

Southern Chicken Salad

* DAIRY-FREE * NUT-FREE

This chicken salad is creamy, flavorful, and the perfect go-to lunch. Kids love its smooth, creamy texture.

1 roasted chicken (5 pounds, or 2.3 kg), meat removed

⅓ to ½ cup (75 to 115 g) mayonnaise or Homemade Mayonnaise (page 68)

Juice of 1 lemon (about 2 to 3 tablespoons [30 to 45 ml])

1 teaspoon Creole Seasoning (optional, page 191)

¼ teaspoon salt

½ teaspoon freshly ground black pepper

½ cup (60 g) finely chopped celery

Grain-free crackers or lettuce, for serving

In a food processor, pulse the chicken a few times to chop roughly. Continue pulsing for about 30 seconds more, or until the chicken is finely chopped. If you let the processor go, your chicken will become a "paste" instead of very finely chopped—don't do this!

In a large bowl, blend together the mayonnaise, lemon juice, Creole Seasoning (if using), salt, and pepper.

Toss in the chicken and stir with a spatula to combine. Throw in the celery and stir again.

Serve with crackers or on top of a bed of lettuce.

YIELD: 6 servings

Chicken Salad-Stuffed Avocado

* DAIRY-FREE * NUT-FREE

We often trade grain-free sandwiches or wraps for a stuffed avocado cup.

1 avocado, halved and pitted

⅓ cup (about 45 g) Southern Chicken Salad (at left)

With a spoon, remove the avocado flesh from each half, dice it small, and place it in a medium bowl. Add the chicken salad and fold together with the avocado.

Spoon half of the avocado-chicken salad mixture into each avocado skin (your "cups") and serve.

YIELD: 2 servings

Arriba! Chunky Chicken Salad

* DAIRY-FREE OPTION * EGG-FREE
* NUT-FREE

The fresh and bold flavors of this chicken salad make eating chicken exciting again.

1 cup (140 g) cooked, chopped, or shredded, chicken

2 celery stalks, finely chopped

¼ cup (65 g) salsa or Homemade Salsa (page 66)

3 tablespoons (7 g) shredded Cheddar cheese (optional)

In a medium bowl, stir together the chicken, celery, salsa, and Cheddar cheese if using. Refrigerate until ready to serve.

YIELD: 2 servings

Almond Chicken Salad

* DAIRY-FREE

This recipe is my version of the almond chicken salad served at one of my favorite restaurants. For the price of a single lunch there, I can feed the whole family.

4 cups (560 g) cooked cubed chicken

1½ cups (225 g) halved seedless grapes

1 cup (100 g) chopped celery

¾ cup (75 g) sliced scallions

3 large hard-boiled eggs, peeled and chopped

½ cup (115 g) mayonnaise or Homemade Mayonnaise (page 68)

1 tablespoon (11 g) Dijon mustard

1 teaspoon salt

½ teaspoon freshly ground black pepper

¼ teaspoon onion powder

¼ teaspoon paprika

½ cup (55 g) slivered almonds, toasted

Chopped kiwi (optional)

In a large bowl, combine the chicken, grapes, celery, scallions, and eggs.

In a small bowl, stir together the mayonnaise, mustard, salt, pepper, onion powder, and paprika until smooth. Pour the dressing over the chicken mixture and toss gently to combine.

Stir in the almonds and serve immediately, or refrigerate for later, adding the almonds just before serving. Garnish with kiwi (if using).

YIELD: 6 to 8 servings

BLT in a Bowl

* DAIRY-FREE OPTION * EGG-FREE
* NUT-FREE

This dish is everything you love about the classic sandwich—but in a bowl. It has all the crunchy textures and salty flavors. It's also perfectly portable to the office for lunch in a container. My kids call these "rainbow" bowls.

6 cups (282 g) finely shredded lettuce

1½ cups (270 g) chopped tomatoes

1 cucumber, thinly sliced

½ cup (60 g) cubed fresh mozzarella (optional)

8 bacon slices, cooked and crumbled

In a large bowl, or four individual serving bowls, layer equal amounts of lettuce, tomatoes, cucumber, mozzarella (if using), and bacon.

Top with your favorite dressing (pages 73 to 74) and serve.

YIELD: 4 servings

Pizza Mini Quiches

* NUT-FREE

Kids love pizza, and what better way to get them excited about lunch than to add the flavors of pizza to a protein-packed mini quiche.

6 large eggs

3 tablespoons (45 ml) milk

1 cup (225 g) pizza toppings of your choice, chopped

1 cup (115 g) shredded cheese of your choice

Preheat the oven to 350°F (180°C) and grease a 24-count mini muffin pan.

In a large bowl, whisk together the eggs and milk. Add the pizza toppings and cheese. Stir to combine.

Evenly divide the egg mixture among the mini muffin cups. Place the pan in the preheated oven and bake for 15 to 18 minutes.

Cool the mini quiches in the pan before carefully removing them with a small knife or spatula.

YIELD: 24 mini quiches

- -

KITCHEN NOTE
I use chopped pepperoni, ham, black olives, and veggies as pizza toppings. The possibilities are endless!

- -

Spinach and Bacon Mini Quiches

*NUT-FREE

These mini quiches are sure to get the kids just as excited about eating their greens as they already are about eating bacon.

Butter or oil, for greasing muffin pan

6 large eggs

3 tablespoons (45 ml) milk

¾ cup (170 g) finely chopped fresh spinach

1 cup (120 g) shredded Cheddar cheese

4 bacon slices, cooked and chopped

Dash of freshly ground black pepper

Preheat the oven to 350°F (180°C) and grease a 24-count mini muffin pan.

In a large bowl, whisk together eggs and milk. Add the spinach, Cheddar cheese, bacon, and pepper. Give it a quick stir to combine the ingredients.

Evenly divide the egg mixture among the mini muffin cups. Place them in the preheated oven and bake for 15 to 18 minutes.

Cool the mini quiches in the pan before carefully removing them with a small knife or spatula.

YIELD: 24 mini quiches

Salsa Mini Quiches

*NUT-FREE

These mini quiches take eggs and salsa to a whole new, portable, level. Make a batch to keep on hand for a healthy snack or on-the-go breakfast option.

Butter or oil, for greasing the muffin pan

6 eggs

3 tablespoons (45 ml) milk

½ cup (130 g) salsa or Homemade Salsa (page 66)

1 cup (120 g) shredded Cheddar cheese

¼ teaspoon salt

¼ teaspoon freshly ground black pepper

Preheat the oven to 350°F (180°C). Grease a 24-count mini muffin pan.

In a large bowl, whisk together the eggs, milk, and salsa. Add the cheese, salt, and pepper. Whisk to combine.

Distribute the egg mixture evenly among the prepared muffin cups. Place them into the preheated oven and bake for 15 to 18 minutes.

Cool the quiches in the pan before carefully removing them with a small knife or spatula.

YIELD: 24 mini quiches

Winter Salad

* DAIRY-FREE OPTION * EGG-FREE
* NUT-FREE

I rarely feel like eating salads in winter but I can't pass up this apple and turkey combination. I hope you love the crunchy mix of textures in this salad as much as my family does.

6 ounces (170 g) spring mix salad, (about 4 large handfuls)

1½ cups (210 g) chopped leftover roasted turkey or chicken

1 medium Granny Smith apple, sliced into thin wedges

1 kiwi, peeled, halved, and sliced into thin pieces

¼ cup (35 g) sunflower seeds

¼ cup (38 g) feta cheese (optional)

¼ to ½ cup (60 to 120 ml) of your favorite dressing (pages 73 to 74)

In a large bowl, combine the spring mix, turkey, apple, kiwi, sunflower seeds, and feta (if using). Evenly divide among 4 plates. Drizzle each with 1 to 2 tablespoons (15 to 30 ml) of your favorite dressing and serve.

YIELD: 4 servings

Rainbow Salad Bar ▷

* DAIRY-FREE OPTION * NUT-FREE OPTION

Colorful salads are more fun to eat, especially when the kids get to build their own bowls.

8 cups (240 g) baby spinach

1 cup (145 g) fresh blueberries

1 cup (145 g) fresh strawberries

1 cup (180 g) orange wedges, cut into chunks

¼ cup (38 g) crumbled feta cheese (optional)

3 large hard-boiled eggs, peeled and sliced

¼ cup (28 g) toasted slivered almonds

¼ to ½ cup (60 to 120 ml) Honey Mustard Vinaigrette (page 73)

Into each of 4 salad bowls arranged in an assembly line, place 2 cups (60 g) of spinach, ¼ cup (36 g) of blueberries, ¼ cup (36 g) of strawberries, ¼ cup (45 g) of orange, 1 tablespoon (9 g) of feta (if using), one-fourth of the egg slices, and 1 tablespoon (7 g) of almonds.

Drizzle each with 1 to 2 tablespoons (15 to 30 ml) of dressing and serve.

YIELD: 4 servings

Allergy Substitution

Use ¼ cup (36 g) toasted sunflower seeds or (16 g) pumpkin seeds instead of almonds.

Mango-Cucumber Salsa

* DAIRY-FREE * EGG-FREE * NUT-FREE

Not just for adults—though I often use this salsa to top a sliced avocado or eat it as is, fresh, with Plantain Chips (page 214)—my daughter loves its sweet and crunchy texture combination.

1 cup (175 g) diced mango

1 cup (135 g) diced cucumber

¼ cup (40 g) diced red onion

¼ cup (4 g) chopped cilantro

1 jalapeño pepper, seeded and diced

Juice of 1 lime

¼ teaspoon salt

⅛ teaspoon pepper

In a medium bowl, stir together the mango, cucumber, red onion, cilantro, jalapeño, lime juice, salt, and pepper.

YIELD: 2 to 4 servings

Laura's Tip

For lunchboxes, halve one avocado and remove the pit. Fill each cavity with salsa and pack one half per lunchbox (squeeze a little additional lime juice on the avocado if you're worried about browning).

Crunchy Turkey Rolls

DAIRY-FREE *EGG-FREE* *NUT-FREE*

Wrapping deli meat in other nutritious ingredients is a great way to make lunch more portable.

8 romaine lettuce leaves, halved lengthwise, stems and center veins removed
8 turkey slices
1 cup (110 g) shredded carrot

On each leaf just below the center, place 1 turkey slice and about 2 tablespoons (14 g) of carrot.

Starting with short side, roll each leaf up and secure with wooden toothpicks.

YIELD: 4 servings

CHAPTER 4
FAMILY MEALS

FROM MY KITCHEN TO YOURS, these are my
family's favorite meals. May they yield endless
joyous moments and many happy plates!

Rosemary Lemon Chicken

* DAIRY-FREE OPTION * EGG-FREE * NUT-FREE

This recipe (and roasting method) is what I use nearly every week because it yields juicy, flavorful, and delicious chicken every time.

1 roasting chicken (5 pounds, or 2.3 kg)

Salt and freshly ground black pepper, to taste

2 or 3 fresh rosemary sprigs

1 lemon, quartered

1 garlic head, top trimmed off, roughly cut

1 to 2 tablespoons (15 to 30 ml) melted butter or olive oil

Vegetable bed, for serving (optional):

1 large onion, sliced

4 to 6 carrots, peeled and cut into 2-inch (5 cm) chunks

1 pound (454 g) Brussels sprouts, halved

Olive oil, for roasting

1½ cups (353 ml) water or chicken stock

Preheat the oven to 425°F (220°C).

Rinse the chicken with cold water inside and out and pat dry with a paper towel. Transfer the chicken to a washable cutting board and remove any excess fat or skin.

Generously season the inside of the chicken with salt and pepper. Stuff the chicken with the rosemary, lemon, and garlic.

With a basting brush, brush the outside of the chicken with the butter and season with salt and pepper.

Using kitchen string, tie the legs together and tuck the wings under the chicken.

Drizzle a roasting pan with olive oil and spread the vegetables (if using) around the pan. Place the chicken in the pan, over the vegetables. Add water or stock to the pan.

Place the pan in the preheated oven and roast the chicken for 1 hour and 15 minutes (a little longer for larger chickens, a little less for smaller), checking for doneness around the breast (165°F [75°C]) and thigh (175°F [80°C]).

Cover a platter or cutting board with aluminum foil. Remove the chicken from the oven, transfer it to the platter, and allow it to rest for 5 to 10 minutes. Transfer the roasted vegetables to the platter and serve.

YIELD: 6 servings

Laura's Tip

Watch how it's made on YouTube.com/MOMables.

Sun-Dried Tomato and Hummus Baked Chicken

* DAIRY-FREE * EGG-FREE * NUT-FREE

One-skillet, 30-minute meals are my favorite. This baked chicken is simple, full of flavor, and delicious. If you've never cooked hummus before, you might want to try it now!

Oil or cooking spray, for greasing the pan

1 large zucchini, sliced

1 large yellow squash, sliced

1 medium onion, chopped

1 tablespoon (15 ml) olive oil

Salt, to taste

Freshly ground black pepper, to taste

4 boneless skinless chicken breasts (6 ounces, or 170 g, each)

1 lemon, thinly sliced

1 cup (246 g) hummus

1 tablespoon (15 g) Sun-Dried-Tomato Pesto (page 129)

Juice of 1 lemon

1 teaspoon smoked paprika

Preheat the oven to 450°F (230°C). Coat a 9 × 9-inch (23 × 23 cm) or 9 × 13-inch (23 × 33 cm) baking dish with oil or cooking spray.

In a large bowl, toss the zucchini, squash, and onion with the olive oil until evenly coated. Season with salt and pepper. Season the chicken breasts with generous pinches of salt and pepper.

Place the vegetables on the bottom of the prepared baking dish to form a base layer. Top with the lemon slices.

In a small bowl, mix together the hummus and pesto.

Place the chicken breasts on top of the vegetables. Cover each breast entirely with the one-fourth of the pesto-hummus mixture.

Sprinkle the lemon juice over the chicken and vegetables. Dust the tops with the smoked paprika.

Place the dish in the preheated oven and bake for 25 to 30 minutes, or until the chicken is cooked through (165°F [75°C]), and the vegetables are tender. Serve immediately.

YIELD: 4 servings

Baked Lemon-Dijon Chicken

★ DAIRY-FREE ★ EGG-FREE ★ NUT-FREE

Full of lemon flavor, this is an easy chicken dish for which the oven does the heavy lifting. I love to pair it with Roasted Beets with Herb-Citrus Dressing (page 199).

1 cup (176 g) Dijon mustard

Juice and zest of 2 lemons

2 tablespoons (30 ml) extra-virgin olive oil

2 tablespoons (4 g) finely chopped fresh rosemary leaves

3 garlic cloves, finely chopped

1 teaspoon crushed red pepper flakes

Pinch of salt

Oil, for greasing the pan

3 pounds (1.4 kg) bone-in split chicken breasts

In a blender, combine the mustard, lemon juice, lemon zest, olive oil, rosemary, garlic, red pepper flakes, and salt.

In a large resealable plastic bag or container, combine the chicken breasts and lemon-Dijon sauce. Refrigerate for 2 hours to marinate, or overnight.

Preheat the oven to 375°F (190°C) and grease a baking pan with oil.

Transfer the marinated chicken breasts into the prepared pan, reserving ¼ cup (60 ml) of the marinade. Place the pan into the preheated oven. Bake for 45 minutes to 1 hour, brushing the chicken with the reserved marinade halfway through, or until the chicken's internal temperature reaches 165°F or (75°C). Remove from the oven and serve.

YIELD: 6 to 8 servings

Almond-Crusted Chicken

* DAIRY-FREE * EGG-FREE

Crunchy, moist, and super-easy. This dish will have everyone asking for more.

Cooking spray, for greasing the pan

1½ pounds (680 g) boneless skinless chicken breasts

½ cup (63 g) almond flour

2 tablespoons (16 g) tapioca flour

½ teaspoon garlic powder

½ teaspoon paprika

¼ teaspoon onion powder

Coconut oil, for cooking

Preheat the oven to 350°F (180°C). Spray a baking pan with cooking spray and set aside.

Cut through the thickness of each chicken breast to butterfly it into two thinner breast filets.

In a gallon-size (3.8 L), resealable plastic bag, combine the almond flour, tapioca flour, garlic powder, paprika, and onion powder. Working with one chicken breast at a time, place it in the resealable bag and shake to coat, while slightly pressing as needed so the coating adheres.

In a large skillet set over medium heat, heat the coconut oil. Panfry the chicken for about 2 minutes, or until golden brown. Flip the chicken and cook the other side for approximately 2 minutes more, or until golden brown and cooked to a safe temperature (165°F [75°C]).

YIELD: 4 servings

Herbed Chicken and Squash

* DAIRY-FREE * EGG-FREE * NUT-FREE

I usually have a few leftover zucchini or squash in the refrigerator at the end of the week. Not wanting to waste them, I use them to form the base for this quick and easy herbed chicken recipe.

4 boneless skinless chicken breast halves (or thighs) (5 ounces, or 141 g, each)

1 tablespoon (3 g) Homemade Italian Seasoning (page 141), crushed

¼ teaspoon salt, plus additional to taste

3 tablespoons (45 ml) olive oil, divided

2 medium yellow squash, diced

2 tablespoons (30 ml) red wine vinegar

1 tablespoon (4 g) snipped fresh dill

¼ teaspoon ground black pepper

Sprinkle the chicken with the Italian seasoning and salt.

In a large skillet set over medium-high heat, heat 1 tablespoon (15 ml) of the olive oil. Add the chicken and cook for about 12 minutes, or until cooked to 165°F (75°C), turning once. Reduce the heat to medium if the chicken browns too quickly. Remove the chicken from the skillet and set aside.

Add the squash to skillet. Cook for about 3 minutes, stirring, until crisp-tender.

Stir in the remaining 2 tablespoons (30 ml) of olive oil, the red wine vinegar, dill, ¼ teaspoon of salt, and pepper. Bring to a simmer, stirring the browned bits from the bottom of the pan. Serve the squash alongside the chicken.

YIELD: 4 servings

Chicken and Chorizo Packets

* DAIRY-FREE OPTION * EGG-FREE * NUT-FREE

I love to cook food in individual "packets" because it's an easy form of kitchen cleanup. After you try it, you'll feel the same way, too!

2 ounces (55 g) dried chorizo (about ½ cup [55 g]), thinly sliced

1 cup (16 g) chopped fresh cilantro

4 scallions, cut into 3-inch (7.5 cm) pieces

3 garlic cloves, roughly chopped

1 small jalapeño pepper, quartered (seeds remove for less heat)

1 tablespoon (4 g) chopped fresh oregano

1 teaspoon cumin seeds

2 tablespoons (30 ml) water

Juice of 1 lime

¼ teaspoon salt

1¾ pounds (795 g) boneless skinless chicken thighs (about 6), halved

1 head of cauliflower, riced (see page 145)

2 red bell peppers, sliced

¼ cup (30 g) shredded Cheddar cheese (optional)

1 lime, cut into 8 wedges

Preheat the oven to 425°F (220°C). Tear off four 12-inch (30 cm) squares of parchment paper.

In a small nonstick skillet set over medium heat, cook the chorizo for about 5 minutes, stirring occasionally, until crisp. With a slotted spoon, transfer to a bowl and set aside. Reserve the drippings and cool slightly.

In a food processor, combine the cilantro, scallions, garlic, jalapeño, oregano, and cumin seeds. Add the water, reserved drippings, lime juice, and salt. Pulse to form a coarse paste. Transfer the paste to a large bowl, add the chicken, and toss to coat.

Divide the riced cauliflower evenly among the 4 parchment squares. Top each with one-fourth of the red bell peppers, chorizo, and chicken. Seal the packets by folding in the top and bottom and lightly twisting the ends together. Divide the packets between 2 baking sheets.

Transfer the sheets to the preheated oven and bake for about 30 minutes, or until the parchment puffs and the chicken is cooked through. Let rest for 5 minutes. Carefully open the packets. Sprinkle with Cheddar cheese (if using), and serve with lime wedges.

YIELD: 4 servings

Braised Short Ribs

* DAIRY-FREE   * EGG-FREE   * NUT-FREE

My mom makes these often for our family meal. The aromas that fill the house are unbelievable. Imagine my happiness to share this recipe with you so you can share it with your family.

5¾ pounds (2.6 kg) bone-in short ribs (about 6)

Salt, to taste

Olive oil, for coating the pan

1 large Spanish onion, cut into ½-inch (1.25 cm) pieces

2 celery stalks, cut into ½-inch (1.25 cm) pieces

2 carrots, peeled, halved lengthwise, then cut into ½-inch (1.25 cm) pieces

2 garlic cloves, smashed

1½ cups (390 g) tomato paste

2 to 3 cups (475 to 710 ml) hearty red wine

2 cups (475 ml) water

1 bunch of fresh thyme, tied with kitchen string

2 bay leaves

Preheat the oven to 375°F (190°C).

Season each short rib generously with salt. Coat an ovenproof pot, large enough to hold all the meat and vegetables, with olive oil. Place it over high heat until hot. Add the short ribs and brown very well, for 2 to 3 minutes per side. Do not overcrowd the pot. Cook them in batches, if necessary.

Meanwhile, in a food processor, purée the onion, celery, carrots, and garlic into a coarse paste.

When the short ribs are browned, remove them from the pot. Drain the fat from the pot and coat the bottom of it again with olive oil.

Add the puréed vegetables to the pot and season generously with salt. Cook for 5 to 7 minutes, browning, or until very dark and a crud has formed on the bottom of the pot. Scrape the crud and let it reform. Scrape the crud again and add the tomato paste. Brown the tomato paste for 4 to 5 minutes.

Add the red wine and scrape the browned bits from the bottom of the pot. Reduce the heat if it starts to burn. Boil the red wine mixture until reduced by half.

Return the short ribs to the pan and add enough of the water just to cover the meat. Add the thyme bundle and bay leaves.

Cover the pot and place it in the preheated oven for 3 hours. Check periodically during the cooking process and add more water, if needed. Turn the ribs over halfway through the cooking time. Remove the lid during the last 20 minutes so things get nice and brown and to reduce the sauce. The meat should be very tender but not falling apart when done. Serve with the braising liquid.

YIELD: 6 to 8 servings

Raspberry-Glazed BBQ Ribs

* DAIRY-FREE * EGG-FREE * NUT-FREE

My mom passed on her love for barbecued ribs to me. This recipe elevates the regular barbecue sauce to that next level, yet it's simple enough to be made without requiring a special occasion. The kids love the finger-licking fun, too.

4 pounds (1.8 kg) pork baby back ribs

¼ cup (60 ml) olive oil

1 teaspoon salt

½ teaspoon freshly ground black pepper

1 cup (235 ml) barbecue sauce

½ cup (160 g) seedless raspberry preserves

½ teaspoon onion powder

¼ teaspoon cayenne pepper

Preheat the oven to 325°F (170°C).

In a small bowl, mix together the olive oil, salt, and pepper. Rub the mixture over both sides of the ribs. Place the ribs in a shallow roasting pan, bone-side down. Cover the pan with aluminum foil and place it in the preheated oven. Bake for 1½ hours, or until the meat begins to feel tender.

In another small bowl, stir together the barbecue sauce, raspberry preserves, onion powder, and cayenne pepper. Reserve ½ cup (120 ml) for serving with the ribs. Brush the ribs with the sauce. Return the ribs to the oven and continue baking, uncovered, for 30 to 40 minutes more, basting the ribs twice during this time.

Once the meat is tender and it separates from the bone, remove from the oven. Serve with the reserved barbecue sauce.

YIELD: 6 to 8 servings

Laura's Tip

Use blueberry or strawberry preserves as an alternative to raspberry. If your family likes it spicy, increase the amount of cayenne pepper, up to ½ teaspoon total.

Lasagna-Stuffed Spaghetti Squash Boats

* DAIRY-FREE OPTION * EGG-FREE * NUT-FREE

I asked my friend, Alison, to share this recipe with me after she told me that her three growing boys practically lick their plates every time she makes it. My family tried the "boats" and thought they were delicious, indeed.

2 teaspoons olive oil

1 cup (160 g) chopped onions

3 garlic cloves, minced

1 pound (455 g) ground beef

¼ pound (115 g) ground pork sausage

2½ teaspoons (2.5 g) Homemade Italian Seasoning (page 141), divided

1 teaspoon salt

1 can (15 ounces, or 425 g) crushed tomatoes

2 medium-size spaghetti squash (about 2½ pounds, or 1 kg each), cooked

1½ cups (375 g) ricotta cheese or Dairy-Free Ricotta Cheese (page 141)

2 tablespoons (8 g) chopped fresh parsley

1 cup (80 g) shredded Romano cheese

Preheat the oven to 400°F (200°C).

To a large skillet set over medium-high heat, add the olive oil. Sauté the onions for about 5 minutes, or until translucent. Add the garlic and cook for 1 minute more.

Add the ground beef, sausage, 1½ teaspoons of Italian seasoning, and salt. Cook for about 8 minutes, breaking up the meat and stirring, or until well browned and no longer pink.

Add the tomatoes and bring the mixture to a simmer. Reduce the heat to low and simmer for 15 minutes.

With a fork, shred the inside of each squash half. Place all four halves into a baking dish (you may need 2). Scoop a generous serving of meat sauce into each squash half and mix with the shredded squash to combine.

In a small dish, stir together the ricotta, remaining 1 teaspoon of Italian seasoning, and parsley. Top each squash half with about ⅓ cup (85 g) of the ricotta mixture. Sprinkle ¼ cup (20 g) of Romano cheese over each half.

Place the pan(s) in the preheated oven and bake for 15 to 20 minutes, or until the tops are golden brown and the ricotta is heated through.

YIELD: 4 generous servings

KITCHEN NOTE

Watch how to cook a spaghetti squash three ways on YouTube.com/MOMables.

Allergy Substitution

I've found that many Romano cheeses are made with goat's milk. This is something my kids can tolerate. If you avoid all dairy proteins completely, omit the cheese.

Greek Steaks

* DAIRY-FREE OPTION * EGG-FREE * NUT-FREE

Each bite of this dish is filled with delicious Mediterranean flavors. I usually pair this meat with a simple vegetable side dish such as spiralized zucchini.

1 lemon

2 boneless beef shoulder top blade (flat iron) steaks (6 ounces, or 170 g, each)

Salt, to taste

Freshly ground black pepper, to taste

1 teaspoon dried rosemary, crushed

2 teaspoons olive oil, divided

1 pint cherry tomatoes, halved

2 garlic cloves, minced

½ cup (50 g) pitted kalamata olives, halved

¼ cup (about 1 ounce [38 g]) crumbled feta cheese (optional)

Zest the lemon and reserve 1 teaspoon of zest. Cut the lemon into 8 wedges and set aside.

Cut each steak in half and generously season both sides with salt and pepper. Sprinkle rosemary evenly over both sides of the steaks and rub it in with your clean fingers.

In a large nonstick skillet set over medium-high heat, heat 1 teaspoon of olive oil. Add the steaks. Cook for 8 to 10 minutes, or until medium, turning once. Remove from the skillet, cover, and keep warm.

To the warm skillet set back over medium-high heat, add the remaining 1 teaspoon of olive oil. Add the tomatoes and garlic. Cook for about 3 minutes, or until the tomatoes start to soften and burst. Remove from the heat. Stir in the olives and reserved 1 teaspoon of lemon zest.

Top each steak with one-fourth of the tomato and olive mixture. Sprinkle each with about 1 tablespoon (9.5 g) of crumbled feta (if using). Serve with the reserved lemon wedges.

YIELD: 4 servings

Laura's Tip

If you have lemon zest remaining after you've added the teaspoon needed for this dish, freeze it in a resealable plastic bag and use it to brighten the flavors of another dish later on.

Olive-Crusted Lamb Chops

* DAIRY-FREE * EGG-FREE * NUT-FREE

My grandmother used to make these on Christmas Eve for our family meal. I hope you enjoy this very dear recipe with your loved ones as much as we continue to do at my house.

1 cup (100 g) pitted kalamata olives

½ of a bunch of fresh oregano, finely chopped

1 garlic clove, smashed

Pinch of crushed red pepper flakes

Extra-virgin olive oil, for creating a paste

One 8-bone (weight will vary) rack of lamb

Olive oil, for browning

Salt, to taste

In a food processor, pulse to combine the olives, oregano, garlic, and red pepper flakes. While the machine is running, drizzle in enough olive oil to create a smooth paste.

Preheat the oven to 425°F (220°C).

Using a sharp knife and working from either end, cut the lamb rack to separate it into individual chops. Season with salt and let it sit at room temperature for 10 to 15 minutes.

Coat a large sauté pan with olive oil and bring it to medium-high heat. Working in batches, add the chops and cook for 2 to 3 minutes per side, turning once, or until beautifully browned. Then, brown the outside edges of each chop.

Place the lamb chops on a baking sheet and top each generously with about 1 tablespoon (16 g) of olive paste. Place the sheet in the preheated oven and roast for 5 to 6 minutes for medium-rare, or 7 to 8 minutes for medium. Remove from the oven and let them rest for 4 to 5 minutes before serving.

YIELD: 8 servings

Laura's Tip

For a budget-friendly option, swap the lamb chops for thick-cut pork chops. Adjust the cooking time until the pork is cooked thoroughly and an internal thermometer reads 145°F (63°C), about 8 minutes, depending on thickness.

Parmesan Pork Chops

*DAIRY-FREE OPTION *EGG-FREE *NUT-FREE

I'm quite sure I won my husband over with this meal many years ago when we were dating. We've been married more than a decade. Now the kids love it, too.

4 boneless center-cut pork chops (6 ounces, or 170 g each), about 1 inch (2.5 cm) thick

Salt and freshly ground black pepper, to taste

2 tablespoons (28 g) coconut oil, divided

¼ cup (25 g) grated Parmesan cheese

½ teaspoon dried oregano

Zest of 1 lemon

1 garlic clove, grated

Juice of 1 lemon

Preheat the oven to 400°F (200°C) and line a baking sheet with aluminum foil.

Season the pork chops with salt and pepper. In a large nonstick skillet set over medium-high heat, heat 1 tablespoon (15 g) of coconut oil. Add the pork chops and sear for 2 to 3 minutes per side, or until golden brown. Transfer to the prepared sheet.

In a small bowl, stir together the Parmesan, oregano, lemon zest, and garlic. Drizzle the lemon juice over the chops and sprinkle the cheese mixture on top. Place them in the preheated oven and bake for about 5 minutes or until just cooked through. Remove from the oven and let rest for 5 minutes before serving.

YIELD: 4 servings

Laura's Tip

I often use Romano cheese instead of Parmesan because it's typically made from goat's milk and my dairy-intolerant child can digest it without much trouble.

Allergy Substitution

Make this dairy-free by substituting 2 tablespoons (10 g) of nutritional yeast combined with ½ teaspoon of paprika for the Parmesan cheese. Sprinkle it lightly over the pork chops along with the other seasonings and follow the rest of the recipe as is.

Salmon Baked in Foil

* DAIRY-FREE * EGG-FREE * NUT-FREE

I am notorious for overcooking nearly every salmon recipe, except this one. With this method, the salmon comes out juicy and tender every time, and it's a family pleaser.

1½ pounds (680 g) salmon, either individual pieces or 1 large fillet

¼ cup (80 g) honey

3 garlic cloves, grated

1 tablespoon (15 ml) olive oil

1 tablespoon (15 ml) white wine vinegar

1 tablespoon (3 g) chopped fresh thyme

¼ teaspoon salt

⅛ teaspoon freshly ground black pepper

Cauliflower rice (page 145), for serving

Preheat the oven to 375°F (190°C) and line a baking sheet with two sheets of aluminum foil, side by side, making the pieces long enough to be able to fold over the salmon to seal. Place the salmon in the center of the foil pieces.

In a small bowl, whisk together the honey, garlic, olive oil, white wine vinegar, thyme, salt, and pepper. Slowly pour the honey mixture over the salmon.

Fold the foil sheets over the salmon and seal them to close. Place the salmon in the preheated oven and bake for 17 to 20 minutes or until the thickest part is no longer pink.

Serve immediately with the cauliflower rice.

YIELD: 4 to 6 servings

Tropical Meatloaf

* DAIRY-FREE * NUT-FREE

Moist and flavorful. This simple and sweet dish will give your family's meatloaf night a little tropical twist.

1½ pounds (680 g) ground chicken or turkey

3 large eggs

1 yellow bell pepper, cut into small dice

¾ cup (132 g) peeled fresh mango chunks, or frozen, thawed

⅓ cup (27 g) unsweetened shredded coconut

¼ cup (15 g) finely chopped fresh parsley

¼ teaspoon crushed red pepper flakes

¼ teaspoon salt

Preheat the oven to 400°F (200°C).

In a large bowl, mix together the chicken, eggs, bell pepper, mango, coconut, parsley, red pepper flakes, and salt. Transfer the mixture to a bread pan. Place it in the preheated oven and bake for 50 to 60 minutes or until the meat is cooked through.

YIELD: 6 servings or 1 loaf

- -

KITCHEN NOTE

You can make the meatloaf mixture ahead of time and freeze it (uncooked). To use, thaw it in the refrigerator for about 24 hours, place it inside a loaf pan, and bake according to recipe's instructions.

- -

Fish from Seville

*DAIRY-FREE *EGG-FREE *NUT-FREE

One bite and I'm back in Spain eating this at a tapas bar with my family. Olé!

4 fresh or frozen skinless tilapia, red snapper, mahimahi, or other white fish (6 to 8 ounces each, or 170 to 225 g each), thawed if frozen

1 tablespoon (15 ml) olive oil

1 cup (160 g) chopped onions

1 garlic clove, minced

1 can (15 ounces, or 425 g) diced tomatoes, with juices

¾ cup (75 g) coarsely chopped pimento-stuffed green olives

1 tablespoon (4 g) snipped fresh oregano or ½ teaspoon dried oregano, crushed

¼ teaspoon salt

⅛ teaspoon freshly ground black pepper

Rinse the fish, pat it dry with paper towels, and set aside.

To a 12-inch (30 cm) skillet set over medium heat, add the olive oil. Add the onion and cook for about 3 minutes, or until translucent. Add the garlic and cook for 1 minute more, or until fragrant. Stir in the tomatoes, olives, oregano, salt, and pepper. Bring the sauce to a boil.

Place the fish on top of the tomato mixture, spooning a few tablespoons (about 45 ml) over the fish. Return the sauce to a boil, reduce the heat to low, and cover. Continue to cook the fish for 8 to 10 minutes more, or until it flakes with a fork.

YIELD: 4 servings

Laura's Tip

Serve with cauliflower rice (page 145).

Mediterranean Cod Pockets

*EGG-FREE *NUT-FREE

I love making these for Sunday meals for my family. Paired with Fennel and Orange Salad (page 77), it's like eating at a fancy restaurant but made simply at home.

For the cod:

1 pound (454 g) small Yukon gold potatoes, thinly sliced, about ⅛ inch (0.3 cm) thick

1 cup (160 g) sliced onions

1 garlic clove, minced

3 tablespoons (45 ml) extra-virgin olive oil, divided

¼ teaspoon crushed red pepper flakes

¼ teaspoon salt, plus additional to taste

4 wild cod fillets (6 ounces, or 170 g each)

2 tablespoons (30 ml) fresh lemon juice

Freshly ground black pepper, to taste

1 teaspoon chopped fresh thyme

¼ cup (25 g) coarsely chopped pitted kalamata olives

1 can (14.5 ounces, or 410 g) petite diced tomatoes

For the chive butter:

2 tablespoons (28 g) unsalted butter or ghee, at room temperature

1 tablespoon (3 g) chopped fresh chives

¼ teaspoon finely grated lemon zest

Pinch of salt

Preheat the oven to 425°F (220°C). Tear off 4 (16-inch [40.6 cm]) sheets of parchment paper.

To make the cod: In a large bowl, toss the potatoes, onions, and garlic with 1 tablespoon (15 ml) of olive oil, the red pepper flakes, and ¼ teaspoon salt.

Put the cod on a plate and drizzle it with lemon juice. Season with salt, pepper, and thyme.

In the middle of 1 sheet of parchment paper, arrange one-fourth of the potato mixture. Top with a cod fillet and one-fourth each of the olives and tomatoes, along with some juice from the can. Drizzle with 1½ teaspoons (7.5 ml) of olive oil. Fold in the sides or the parchment and twist the ends to seal the ingredients in a "pocket."

Repeat the process with the remaining ingredients. Place 2 finished "pockets" on each of 2 baking sheets. Place the sheets in the preheated oven and bake for about 25 minutes, or until the parchment puffs and the liquid bubbles. Remove from the oven and let rest for 5 minutes before opening.

To make the chive butter: While the fish cooks, in a small bowl, mix together the butter, chives, lemon zest, and salt.

Carefully open the pockets, top each with chive butter, and serve.

YIELD: 4 servings

Braised Chicken Thighs with Carrots and Potatoes

* EGG–FREE * NUT–FREE

Crispy on the outside and perfectly juicy on the inside, this is one meal you'll want to make often.

1½ pounds (680 g) boneless skinless chicken thighs, fat trimmed

Salt and freshly ground black pepper, to taste

Sweet paprika, to taste

2 tablespoons (28 g) butter or ghee

1 red onion, finely chopped

1 pound (455 g) red-skinned potatoes, about 2 inches (5 cm) in diameter, quartered

8 carrots, halved lengthwise and cut into 1½-inch (3.75 cm) pieces

1 tablespoon (8 g) tapioca starch

1⅓ cups (315 ml) low-sodium chicken broth

⅓ cup (80 ml) dry vermouth or dry white wine

1½ tablespoons (4 g) minced fresh thyme

Season the chicken lightly with salt and pepper and generously with paprika. In a heavy large frying pan set over medium-high heat, warm the butter. Add the chicken and cook for about 2 minutes per side, until brown. Transfer the chicken to a plate and set aside.

In the pan, stir together the onion, potatoes, and carrots. Sprinkle with salt and pepper. Sauté for about 5 minutes, or until the vegetables begin to brown. Add the tapioca starch and stir to coat.

Gradually stir in the chicken broth and vermouth. Bring to a boil, stirring frequently. Return the chicken to the pan and bring to a boil again.

Cover the pan, reduce the heat to medium-low, and simmer for about 25 minutes, or until the chicken and vegetables are cooked through. Stir and turn the chicken over occasionally.

Stir in the thyme. Adjust the seasonings to taste. Divide the chicken and vegetables among 4 warmed plates and serve immediately.

YIELD: 4 servings

Clams with Chorizo

EGG-FREE *NUT-FREE*

I grew up eating clams fresh from the bay at my grandparents' home. They are a nutritionally dense protein that is high in iron and minerals. Serve these with Smoky Cauliflower (page 182) for a complete meal.

1 tablespoon (15 ml) olive oil

8 ounces (225 g) Spanish-style dried chorizo, sliced into thin rounds

1 small onion, diced

Pinch crushed red pepper flakes

1 garlic clove, minced

24 cockles or small clams, cleaned

¼ cup (60 ml) bottled clam juice

½ cup (120 ml) dry white wine

1 tablespoon (14 g) unsalted butter

1 tablespoon (4 g) finely chopped fresh parsley

Salt and freshly ground black pepper, to taste

In a large sauté pan, preferably one that can also be used for serving, set over high heat, heat the olive oil. When it begins to smoke, add the chorizo and cook for about 2 minutes, until just beginning to color. Add the onion and red pepper flakes and cook for about 2 minutes more, stirring, until the onion is translucent.

Add the garlic, cockles, clam juice, and white wine. Reduce the heat to medium and cook for 5 to 7 minutes, until the cockles open and are warmed through. Discard any cockles that do not open.

Remove from the heat and stir in the butter and parsley. Season with salt and pepper.

YIELD: 4 servings

Baked Cod

DAIRY-FREE *EGG-FREE* *NUT-FREE*

Growing up in Spain, baked cod was a weekly fish staple at our house. If you can't find cod, use any white fish your family enjoys.

4 thick cod, flounder, or pollock fillets

¼ cup (60 ml) olive oil, plus more for brushing

8 thin lemon slices, divided

Salt and freshly ground black pepper, to taste

¼ cup (15 g) chopped fresh parsley

2 tablespoons (12 g) chopped fresh mint

Juice of ½ of a lemon

1 garlic clove, crushed

Preheat the oven to 400°F (200°C). Tear off 4 parchment squares, each large enough to encase 1 fillet in a package.

Rinse each fish fillet, pat dry with paper towel, and brush with oil. Place each fillet on a parchment paper square.

Top each fillet with 2 lemon slices, and season with salt and pepper. Fold over the parchment to encase and twist the ends to seal. Place the packets in the preheated oven and bake for 20 minutes, or until just cooked through and opaque.

Meanwhile, in a food processor, combine ¼ cup (60 ml) of olive oil, the parsley, mint, lemon juice, and garlic. Process until finely chopped. Season with salt and pepper.

Place each package on a serving plate and carefully unfold the parchment. Top each piece of fish with a spoonful of herb sauce before serving.

YIELD: 4 servings

Coconut Shrimp with Tropical Rice

★ DAIRY–FREE ★ NUT–FREE

This is one of my husband's favorite recipes reinvented to this grain-free version that now our whole family can enjoy. The Tropical Rice is what I often pair with this shrimp.

Nonstick cooking spray

For the tropical rice:

3 cups (372 g) cauliflower rice (see page 145)

Zest of 1 lime

½ cup (55 g) shredded carrots

2 tablespoons (20 g) finely chopped red onion or scallion

¼ teaspoon salt

Freshly ground black pepper, to taste

For the coconut shrimp:

2 large eggs

2 tablespoons (16 g) tapioca starch

2 cups (160 g) unsweetened shredded coconut

¼ cup (32 g) coconut flour

½ teaspoon paprika

Salt, to taste

⅓ cup (75 g) coconut oil, plus additional as needed

2 pounds (908 g) shrimp, peeled and deveined

2 tablespoons (2 g) chopped fresh cilantro

1 lime, cut into 8 wedges

Preheat the oven to 420°F (215.5°C). Line a rimmed baking sheet with aluminum foil and set a wire rack on top. Coat the rack with cooking spray.

To make the tropical rice: In a large skillet set over medium heat, stir together the cauliflower rice and lime zest. Add in—but do not stir—the carrots, red onion, salt, and a few grinds of pepper. Cover and let sit for 10 minutes, then fluff with a fork to combine. Transfer to a large bowl and set aside.

To make the coconut shrimp: Gather two small bowls. In one, whisk together the eggs and tapioca starch. In the second, stir together the coconut, coconut flour, and paprika. Season with salt.

Butterfly your shrimp by slicing them down the back until they open up and can almost lie flat. You can leave the tails on, which I do to make flipping and eating easier.

Place the same large skillet that you cooked the rice in over medium heat and melt the coconut oil.

Working one at a time, dip each shrimp into the egg wash, letting the excess fall off, and then dredge it through the coconut mixture.

Fry the shrimp in batches for 2 to 3 minutes per side, or until opaque in the center and golden brown on the outside. Do not overcrowd the pan. If the pan runs out of oil, add 1 or 2 more tablespoons (14 to 28 g) before cooking the next batch. Transfer the cooked shrimp to a paper towel–lined plate to drain.

Add the cilantro to the rice mixture and toss to combine. Serve with the shrimp and lime wedges.

YIELD: 4 servings

Midweek Paella

* DAIRY-FREE * EGG-FREE * NUT-FREE

Being from Spain, I consider paella a mealtime staple. When I was able to re-create the dish to be grain-free, I was thrilled. Most importantly, the dish comes together in about 30 minutes, making it a great option for a weeknight dinner.

12 ounces (340 g) chicken thigh fillets, cut into 1-inch (2.5 cm) pieces

Salt and freshly ground black pepper, to taste

1 tablespoon (15 ml) olive oil

2 garlic cloves, minced

1 small yellow onion, diced

6 ounces (165 g) chorizo, quartered vertically, and then diced into ⅓-inch (8 mm) pieces

1 small red bell pepper, roughly diced

1 can (14.5 ounces, or 410 g) crushed tomatoes

1 cauliflower head (about 4 cups [400 g]), riced (see method, page 145)

2 cups (65 g) packed finely chopped spinach

⅓ cup (43 g) frozen peas

1 teaspoon paprika

1½ tablespoons (6 g) finely chopped parsley

Season the chicken with salt and pepper.

In a large pan set over medium-high heat, heat the olive oil. Sear the chicken until all sides are golden brown and nearly cooked through. It will continue to cook with the remaining ingredients. Transfer the chicken to a plate and set aside.

Add the garlic, onion, and chorizo to the pan. The chorizo will release oil so you don't need to add more to the pan. Cook for 1 minute, stirring, until the chorizo starts to brown. Add the red bell pepper and cook for 1 minute more, or until the chorizo is dark golden brown. Return the chicken to the pan.

Add the crushed tomatoes, cauliflower rice, spinach, frozen peas, and paprika. Stir to combine and cook for about 5 minutes, or until the cauliflower is tender.

Garnish with parsley and serve.

YIELD: 6 servings

Shrimp Scampi with Spaghetti Squash

* EGG-FREE   * NUT-FREE

Shrimp scampi is the type of recipe I pull together when I have no time to cook. For that reason alone, I keep an emergency stash in the freezer at all times. Here, spaghetti squash stands in for the traditional pasta, but you won't miss it at all.

2 tablespoons (28 g) butter or ghee	**Pinch of crushed red pepper flakes (optional)**
1 pound (454 g) raw shrimp, peeled and deveined	**2 tablespoons (30 ml) fresh lemon juice**
Dash of salt	**Minced fresh parsley, for garnish**
3 garlic cloves, minced	**1 medium spaghetti squash, cooked and shredded**

In a large pan set over medium heat, melt the butter. Add the shrimp and salt. Sauté for about 3 minutes, turning at least once.

Add the garlic and red pepper flakes (if using) and cook for about 3 minutes more, or until the shrimp are cooked through.

Add the lemon juice, sprinkle with parsley, toss to combine, and remove from the heat immediately.

Serve over shredded spaghetti squash.

YIELD: 4 servings

Laura's Tip

Cook the spaghetti squash up to 3 days prior to when you plan to prepare this recipe. Shred the squash with a fork and refrigerate it in a sealed container. Alternately, you can use cooked cauliflower rice (page 145) as a base.

Grain-Free Tortillas

* DAIRY-FREE * EGG-FREE * NUT-FREE OPTION

This simple recipe will forever revolutionize your taco night, guaranteed.

1 cup (125 g) packed almond flour, plus additional as needed

½ cup (65 g) packed tapioca flour

¼ teaspoon salt

¼ teaspoon ground cumin (optional)

3 tablespoons (45 ml) avocado oil or olive oil

3 tablespoons (45 ml) warm water, plus additional as needed

In a medium bowl, whisk together the almond flour, tapioca flour, salt, and cumin (if using). Add the avocado oil and stir to combine. Slowly add the water, 1 tablespoon (15 ml) at a time, and knead with your clean hands to combine.

Transfer the dough to a flat surface and knead for about 1 minute. If the dough is too wet, add a little more almond flour. If too dry, add a teaspoon or two of water. The dough's texture will vary depending on how you measure the flour. It should feel like play dough. Divide the dough evenly into 8 pieces total. Knead and roll each piece into a small ball.

Meanwhile, place a large skillet over medium heat.

Place 1 dough ball between two pieces of parchment paper. With a rolling pin or tortilla press, flatten or roll the dough into a 6-inch (15 cm) tortilla.

Peel off the top piece of parchment and flip the tortilla into the hot skillet, pulling away the second piece of parchment as you do so. Cook the first side for about 20 seconds, or until it begins to brown. Flip the tortilla over and cook the other side for 30 to 45 seconds, or until the other side is browned and bubbly.

Immediately transfer the warm tortilla to a tortilla warmer or place it between two clean kitchen towels to keep warm. These tortillas are best served warmed. Refrigerate any leftover tortillas. To enjoy again, simply warm them in the toaster oven until soft and pliable. Times will vary depending on your oven.

YIELD: 8 tortillas

Allergy Substitution

No-Nut Flour (page 32) will work as an almond flour substitute for this recipe. Coconut flour will not work, as it's not a 1:1 substitute.

Laura's Tip

I use a large skillet so I can cook 4 to 6 tortillas at a time. Working quickly is a must because they are most pliable when warm.

Grilled Fish Tacos with Lime-Cabbage Slaw

*DAIRY-FREE *EGG-FREE *NUT-FREE OPTION

I nearly always order fish tacos when I go out to eat so it's no wonder I included it in this book for you and your family. Enjoy!

3 tablespoons (45 ml) olive oil, divided

3 tablespoons (45 ml) fresh lime juice, divided

1 garlic clove, minced

1 teaspoon chili powder

½ teaspoon ground cumin

½ teaspoon paprika

⅛ teaspoon salt

⅛ teaspoon freshly ground black pepper

1 pound (454 g) tilapia, cod, or mahimahi fillets

Cooking oil, for cooking

1 small bag (6 ounces, or 170 g) coleslaw mix

¼ cup (4 g) chopped cilantro

½ of a red onion, thinly sliced

1 large avocado, peeled, pitted, and sliced

6 Grain-Free Tortillas (page 124), warmed

In a small bowl, whisk together 1½ tablespoons (23 ml) of olive oil, 1½ tablespoons (23 ml) of lime juice, the garlic, chili powder, cumin, paprika, salt, and pepper.

Place the fish into a gallon-size (3.8 L) resealable plastic bag and pour the marinade in over the fish. Seal the bag, turn to coat, and refrigerate for at least 30 minutes.

Preheat a grill or large skillet to medium-high heat and brush the grill grates with cooking oil. Place the fish on the grill. Cook for about 3 minutes per side, or until cooked through. (The exact cook time will vary based on the thickness of your fish.)

Meanwhile, in a medium bowl, combine the slaw, cilantro, and onion. Sprinkle the remaining 1½ tablespoons (23 ml) of olive oil and 1½ tablespoons (23 ml) of lime juice over it and season lightly with salt and pepper. Toss to coat evenly.

Transfer the fish to a plate and break it into pieces. Build each taco by placing grilled fish, avocado slices, and slaw on top of each tortilla. (Note: See nut-free option for tortillas on page 124.)

YIELD: 4 servings

Italian Turkey Burgers

* DAIRY-FREE * EGG-FREE * NUT-FREE

When my husband mentioned that turkey burgers are often kind of bland, I decided to upgrade my basic recipe. This is a definite improvement that should banish the bland from your mealtime.

5 ounces (140 g) finely chopped spinach

1 pound (454 g) ground turkey

1½ teaspoons Homemade Italian Seasoning (page 141)

½ teaspoon garlic powder

½ teaspoon salt

Large lettuce leaves, for serving

4 tablespoons (60 g) Sun-Dried-Tomato Pesto (at right)

1 recipe of Carrot French Fries (page 170)

In a large bowl, combine the spinach, turkey, Italian seasoning, garlic powder, and salt until blended.

Divide the mixture into 4 pieces and shape into patties. Gently press down the center of each patty to create a slight depression so the burger will cook evenly.

Preheat the grill to medium high, or place a large skillet over medium-high heat. Cook for about 4 minutes per side, or until the internal temperature reaches 165°F (75°C). Serve over large lettuce leaves. Top each with 1 tablespoon (15 g) of Sun-Dried-Tomato Pesto and your favorite burger toppings.

Serve with the Carrot French Fries.

YIELD: 4 burgers

Sun-Dried Tomato Pesto

* DAIRY-FREE OPTION * EGG-FREE
* NUT-FREE OPTION

From topping plain burgers to upgrading spiralized veggies, this Sun-Dried-Tomato Pesto is one you'll want to have in your fridge for just about any meal.

½ cup (55 g) oil-packed sun-dried tomatoes, drained

¼ cup (25 g) grated Romano cheese

¼ cup (30 g) walnuts

1 small garlic clove

2 tablespoons (30 ml) extra-virgin olive oil

Salt, to taste

In a food processor, pulse together the sun-dried tomatoes, Romano cheese, walnuts, and garlic until blended. With the processor running, slowly add the olive oil. Season with salt.

YIELD: About 1 cup (145 g)

Allergy Substitution

Substitute sunflower seeds or pumpkin seeds for the walnuts for a nut-free version. If you need a dairy-free alternative, omit the Romano and add some additional nuts or seeds to thicken the pesto. Even without the cheese, the flavor of this thick paste is delicious.

Turkey Marsala with Lemon-Butter Broccolini

EGG-FREE *NUT-FREE*

Since chicken dishes can often feel a little "routine," I've switched up the classic Chicken Marsala recipe to be made with turkey. The Lemon-Butter Broccolini (page 185) adds some beautiful color and a bright taste to the plate.

1½ pounds (680 g) turkey cutlets, pounded thin (about ¼ inch [6 mm] thick)

Salt, to taste

¼ cup (33 g) tapioca flour

¼ cup (60 ml) olive oil

2 bacon slices, chopped into small pieces

8 ounces (226 g) cremini mushrooms, stemmed and halved

½ cup (120 ml) sweet Marsala wine

½ cup (120 ml) chicken broth

2 tablespoons (28 g) unsalted butter or ghee

Parsley, for garnish

Lemon-Butter Broccolini (page 185), for serving

Season the turkey cutlets generously with salt.

On a shallow platter, distribute the tapioca flour. Dredge the turkey cutlets generously in the flour to coat both sides.

In a large skillet set over medium-high heat, heat the olive oil. Once the oil is hot, fry the cutlets for about 5 minutes per side, or until golden, working in batches if needed. Transfer cutlets to a plate and set aside. Reduce the heat under the skillet to medium.

Add the bacon pieces to the leftover turkey oil and cook for about 1 minute to release some of the bacon fat. Add the mushrooms and sauté for about 4 minutes, or until browned.

Pour the Marsala into the pan and bring it to a boil. Reduce the heat to low and simmer for about 1 minute to cook off most of the alcohol. Add the chicken broth, and continue to simmer for 1 minute more.

Add the butter to melt. Return the turkey cutlets to the pan. Simmer for about 1 minute to heat through. Garnish with parsley and serve with the broccolini.

YIELD: 4 servings

Korean Beef Bowls

* DAIRY-FREE * EGG-FREE * NUT-FREE

Made with ground beef for a more budget-friendly family meal option, this Korean Beef beats your typical takeout in both flavor and cost!

⅓ cup (80 ml) coconut aminos

2½ tablespoons (50 g) honey

2 tablespoons (30 ml) sesame oil

3 garlic cloves, minced

1 tablespoon (6 g) grated fresh ginger

1 bunch scallions, chopped, white and green parts separated

½ teaspoon freshly ground black pepper

½ teaspoon chili paste (Sriracha)

2 tablespoons (30 ml) cooking oil

1½ pounds (680 g) ground beef

1 tablespoon (9 g) toasted sesame seeds (optional)

3 to 4 cups (500 to 675 g) cauliflower rice (page 145)

1 pound (454 g) broccoli florets, steamed

In a small bowl, stir together the coconut aminos, honey, sesame oil, garlic, ginger, white scallion parts, pepper, and chili paste.

In a large skillet set over medium-high heat, heat the cooking oil. Brown the meat for 5 to 8 minutes, breaking it up with a spatula as it cooks. Continue cooking until the meat is no longer pink. Add the sauce to the skillet, bringing it to a quick boil, and then reduce the heat to low. Cover and simmer for about 4 minutes.

Serve warm, sprinkled with the green scallion tops and sesame seeds (if using) over the cauliflower rice with steamed broccoli on the side.

YIELD: 4 servings

Quick Mu Shu Pork

* DAIRY-FREE * EGG-FREE * NUT-FREE

Quick, delicious, and easy. This is my favorite dish at our local Chinese takeout. I could eat it for days and still love it. By changing up the protein (try chicken or shrimp), you'll never get tired of it!

2 tablespoons (28 g) coconut oil, divided

12 ounces (340 g) boneless pork loin chops, cut into ¼-inch (6 mm) strips

8 ounces (225 g) fresh button mushrooms, sliced

½ cup (75 g) diagonally sliced scallions

4 cups (360 g) packaged coleslaw mix

2 tablespoons (30 ml) coconut aminos

1 teaspoon toasted sesame oil

⅛ teaspoon crushed red pepper flakes

In a large skillet or wok set over medium-high heat, heat 1 tablespoon (28 g) of coconut oil. Add the pork and cook for about 3 minutes, stirring, to brown all the edges. Once the pork is no longer pink, remove it from the skillet.

Add the remaining 1 tablespoon (28 g) of coconut oil to the warm skillet and sauté the mushrooms and scallions. Cook for 2 to 3 minutes, or until the mushrooms are tender. Add the coleslaw mix and carrots. Cook for 2 minutes more, or until the cabbage wilts.

Meanwhile, in a small bowl, stir together the coconut aminos, sesame oil, and red pepper flakes.

Return the pork to the skillet. Pour the sauce over the pork and stir to combine.

Enjoy as is or serve over steamed cauliflower rice (page 145) or inside a Grain-Free Tortilla (page 124).

YIELD: 4 servings

Buffalo and Kale Tacos

* DAIRY-FREE * EGG-FREE * NUT-FREE OPTION

Wendi Humes, a MOMables community member, shared this recipe with me. It's one of her family's favorite taco recipes, and it includes kale! I promised her son I'd include it in my next book and make a video. So here it is!

1 tablespoon (14 g) coconut oil

½ pound (227 g) ground grass-fed buffalo

½ cup (55 g) grated carrot

½ cup (80 g) diced onion

2 garlic cloves, finely chopped

½ teaspoon salt

1 tablespoon (8 g) mild chili powder

1 teaspoon ground cumin

2 tablespoons (32 g) tomato paste

2 cups (134 g) kale leaves, thoroughly washed and sliced into thin strips

½ cup (120 ml) water

Sliced avocados or Easy Guacamole (page 71), for garnish

Salsa or Homemade Salsa (page 66), for garnish

In a large skillet set over medium-high heat, add the coconut oil. Once heated, add the ground buffalo meat, carrot, onion, and garlic. Cook for about 5 minutes, breaking up the meat with a spoon, or until the meat begins to brown and the veggies soften.

Stir in the salt, chili powder, cumin, and tomato paste. Add the kale and toss to combine. Stir in the water. Reduce the heat to low and simmer for about 5 minutes, or until the kale softens.

Serve over cauliflower rice (page 145) or scoop into warm Grain-Free Tortillas (page 124). Top with guacamole and salsa. Note: The recipe will not be nut-free if using the tortillas.

YIELD: 4 servings

- -

KITCHEN NOTE

Ground buffalo meat is very lean and, therefore, no draining of "fat" is necessary for this recipe. You can also use ground beef or turkey as a substitute.

- -

Laura's Tip

See how this recipe is made on YouTube.com/MOMables.

Creamy Thai Chicken

*DAIRY-FREE *EGG-FREE *NUT-FREE

The semester I lived in New York City as an undergraduate student I ate my fair share of Thai delivery. This recipe is one of my favorites and kept me nourished for late-night studying. It now nourishes my family—and yours.

2 tablespoons (28 g) coconut oil, divided

1 pound (454 g) boneless skinless chicken breasts, cubed

4 scallions, sliced, white and green parts separated

1 tablespoon (6 g) minced fresh ginger

1 package (1 pound, or 454 g) butternut squash cubes

1 can (14 ounces, or 425 ml) coconut milk

¾ cup (175 ml) water

2 tablespoons (30 ml) fresh lime juice

1½ tablespoons (25 ml) Asian fish sauce or coconut aminos

1 tablespoon (16 g) Thai red curry paste

2 tablespoons (25 g) coconut palm sugar

3 cups (375 g) cooked cauliflower rice (page 145), divided

⅓ cup (13 g) sliced fresh basil

In a large skillet set over medium-high heat, warm 1 tablespoon (14 g) of coconut oil. Cook the chicken for about 5 minutes, or until it is no longer pink inside. Transfer the chicken to a plate and set aside.

In a heavy, medium pot set over medium-low heat, warm the remaining 1 tablespoon (14 g) of coconut oil. Add the white scallion parts and the ginger. Cook, stirring, for about 2 minutes, or until fragrant.

Add the squash and stir for 1 minute to heat through.

Stir in the coconut milk, water, lime juice, fish sauce, curry paste, and coconut palm sugar and bring to a simmer.

Stir in the chicken. Partially cover the skillet and simmer for about 20 minutes, or until the squash is just tender.

Put ¾ cup (94 g) of cauliflower rice into each of 4 warmed bowls. Spoon the curry chicken over, top with the green scallion parts and basil, and serve immediately.

YIELD: 4 servings

Veggie Fried Rice

* DAIRY-FREE * NUT-FREE

When that craving for Chinese takeout hits, be prepared to satisfy it with this homemade version instead. If you need the takeout experience, serve it in paper cartons with chopsticks for a family-fun dinner tonight.

2 large eggs, lightly beaten

2 tablespoons (30 ml) plus 1 teaspoon coconut aminos, divided

1 teaspoon toasted sesame oil or vegetable oil

1 garlic clove, minced

1 tablespoon (14 g) coconut oil, plus additional as needed

½ cup (50 g) thinly bias-sliced celery (about 1 stalk)

¾ cup (52.5 g) sliced fresh mushrooms

3 cups (375 g) cooked cauliflower rice (page 145)

1 medium carrot cut into thin, bite-size strips or ½ cup (30 g) packaged fresh julienned carrots

½ cup (65 g) frozen peas, thawed

¼ cup (57.5 g) sliced scallions

In a small bowl, whisk the eggs with 1 teaspoon of coconut aminos and set aside.

In a large skillet or wok set over medium heat, heat the sesame oil. Add the garlic and cook, stirring, for 30 seconds. Add the eggs and cook, stirring gently, until set. Remove from the heat. Remove the cooked egg from skillet, roll it into a log, and cut it into strips.

Add the coconut oil to the skillet and place it over medium-high heat. Add the celery and cook for 1 minute, stirring. Add the mushrooms and cook for 1 to 2 minutes more, stirring, until the vegetables are crisp-tender. Add more coconut oil to the pan, as needed, during cooking.

Add the cauliflower rice, carrot, and peas to the skillet. Drizzle with the remaining 2 tablespoons (30 ml) of coconut aminos. Cook for 4 to 6 minutes, stirring, or until heated through. Add the egg strips and scallions. Cook for about 1 minute more, stirring, or until the egg strips are heated through.

YIELD: 4 servings

Shrimp Pad Thai

*DAIRY-FREE *EGG-FREE *NUT-FREE

Shrimp Pad Thai is another one of my favorite takeout recipes. This easy recipe comes together faster than the delivery man can get to my door to feed my hungry family.

1 tablespoon (6 g) curry seasoning

1 can (14 ounces, or 425 ml) coconut milk

¼ teaspoon salt

¼ teaspoon freshly ground black pepper

1 pound (454 g) uncooked shrimp, fresh or frozen, thawed, peeled, and deveined

4 medium zucchini, spiralized

½ cup (8 g) fresh minced cilantro

Lime wedges, for serving (optional)

In a large skillet set over medium heat, toast the curry powder for about 1 minute, or until aromatic. Stir in the coconut milk, salt, and pepper. Bring to a boil. Add the shrimp and cook for 4 to 5 minutes, or until the shrimp begin to turn pink.

Add the zucchini noodles and toss to coat with the sauce. Cook for 3 minutes more, or until the zucchini noodles soften but still have a slightly crisp texture.

Sprinkle with cilantro and serve each portion with a lime wedge (if using).

YIELD: 4 servings

Portobello-Stuffed Pizzas

* DAIRY-FREE OPTION * EGG-FREE * NUT-FREE OPTION

A nutrient-dense pizza? Yes! These individual pizzas are fun to make and easy to customize, making veggies that much more fun to eat!

6 ounces (170 g) tomato paste

¼ cup (60 ml) water

6 large fresh portobello mushrooms

**2 tablespoons (10 g) Parmesan cheese or 2 tablespoons (24 g) nutritional yeast plus
½ teaspoon ground cumin, divided**

1½ cups (375 g) Dairy-Free Ricotta Cheese (page 141), divided

Your favorite pizza toppings

Preheat the oven to 375°F (190°C). Place a cooling rack on top of a baking sheet and set aside. This allows the portobello juices to drip down to the pan without making the mushrooms soggy.

In a small bowl, mix together the tomato paste and water.

If you are not using the Parmesan, in another small bowl, stir together the nutritional yeast and cumin.

If you prefer, use a spoon to scrape the gills from the mushrooms. Spread equal amounts of the tomato paste onto each mushroom. Top each with about ¼ cup (65 g) of the ricotta and sprinkle about 1 teaspoon of Parmesan (if using), or nutritional yeast mixture, over each.

Add your favorite toppings as you'd normally add to any pizza.

Place the pizzas on the rack and put the sheet in the preheated oven. Bake for 20 to 25 minutes, or until a fork poking the side of a mushroom goes through without any resistance and the tops are light golden brown.

YIELD: 6 servings

Allergy Substitution

If dairy is not a concern but nuts are, use regular ricotta cheese for this recipe and omit the nutritional yeast and cumin. Sprinkle a bit of sharp Cheddar cheese on top for added flavor. (Note that the Dairy-Free Ricotta Cheese contains cashews.)

Baked Ranch Chicken Wings

* EGG-FREE * DAIRY-FREE * NUT-FREE OPTION

These are perfect to serve on game day or for a homemade version of the classic restaurant favorite when you want mealtime to feel more like party time.

1 tablespoon (9 g) plus 1 teaspoon onion powder

1 tablespoon (9 g) garlic powder

1½ teaspoons dried dill

¼ teaspoon salt

¼ teaspoon freshly ground black pepper

¼ cup (60 ml) coconut milk

1¼ cups (295 ml) almond milk

3 pounds (1.4 kg) chicken wings, split at the joints

1 small onion, sliced into thick rings

Oil, for cooking and greasing the baking sheet

In a small bowl, combine the onion powder, garlic powder, dill, salt, and pepper. Transfer to an airtight container.

Into a large resealable plastic bag, pour the coconut milk and almond milk. Add 2 teaspoons of the onion-garlic seasoning blend, the chicken wings, and onion rings. Seal the bag, turn to coat, and refrigerate for at least 2 hours, or overnight.

Preheat the oven to 425°F (220°C) and grease a baking sheet with oil.

Remove the wings from the marinade and place them on the prepared sheet. Discard the marinating liquid and onions. Sprinkle the remaining 2 tablespoons (18 g) plus 1 teaspoon of seasoning over the wings and place them in the preheated oven. Bake for 40 to 45 minutes, or until browned and crisp.

Remove from the oven and serve with Homemade Ranch Dressing (page 74).

YIELD: 8 servings

Allergy Substitution

Use a nut-free milk of your choice instead of the almond milk.

Homemade Italian Seasoning

* DAIRY-FREE * EGG-FREE * NUT-FREE

While many of us have a jar of Italian seasoning in our pantries, it's nice to have a recipe and make your own, fresh, at any time.

2 tablespoons (4 g) dried basil

2 tablespoons (6 g) dried oregano

2 tablespoons (7 g) dried rosemary

2 tablespoons (3.5) dried marjoram

2 tablespoons (6 g) dried thyme

1 tablespoon (9 g) garlic powder

2 teaspoons crushed red pepper flakes (optional)

In a food processor or spice grinder, combine the basil, oregano, rosemary, marjoram, thyme, garlic, and red pepper flakes (if using). Give it a quick pulse to break up the dried leaves into uniform pieces.

YIELD: About ½ cup (50 g)

Dairy-Free Ricotta Cheese

* DAIRY-FREE * NUT-FREE OPTION

There are lots of nut-cheese recipes around the web, so I realize that you might already have your favorite. If not, try this to see if it fills the need.

1½ cups (225 g) raw cashews, soaked in water with ¾ teaspoon of salt for 4 hours, or overnight

¼ cup (60 ml) plus 2 teaspoons water, divided

3 tablespoons (45 ml) olive oil

2 tablespoons (30 ml) plus 1 teaspoon fresh lemon juice

Drain and rinse the cashews. Add them to a food processor or blender along with ¼ cup (60 ml) of water, the olive oil, and lemon juice. Pulse to combine and process until smooth and the texture resembles ricotta cheese. If it's too thick, slowly add the remaining 2 teaspoons of water until it reaches your desired texture.

Keep refrigerated for up to 5 days.

YIELD: About 1 cup (225 g)

Allergy Substitution

I've tried this recipe using sunflower seeds many times. The color will not be white like real ricotta cheese or this cashew version, but it's a good nut-free alternative.

Laura's Tip

When using this substitute in Italian recipes, such as the Portobello- Stuffed Pizzas (page 139), add 1 teaspoon of Homemade Italian Seasoning (page 141) for added flavor.

Skillet Teriyaki Chicken

★ DAIRY-FREE ★ EGG-FREE ★ NUT-FREE

This is one family meal that everyone eats without a fuss. The classic flavors come to life in this easy-to-make teriyaki sauce.

1½ pounds (680 g) boneless skinless chicken breasts or thighs

¼ cup (80 g) honey or coconut palm sugar

½ cup (120 ml) coconut aminos

1 small garlic clove, grated

¼ teaspoon grated fresh ginger

Oil, for cooking

Pound the chicken to ¼ inch (6 mm) by starting in the middle and working out to the edges. Place the chicken into a glass container or large, gallon-size (3.8 L) resealable plastic bag.

In a medium bowl, whisk together the honey, coconut aminos, garlic, and ginger. Add the sauce to the chicken and mix a few times to combine. Refrigerate the chicken for 30 minutes to 2 hours to marinate, or overnight for a stronger flavor.

In a large skillet set over medium heat, heat enough oil to cover the bottom of the pan. Add the chicken, in batches if needed, and cook for about 3 minutes per side. Reserve the marinade. Remove the chicken from the pan and set aside

Pour the reserved marinade into the pan. Bring it to a boil, reduce the heat to low, and simmer for about 2 minutes. Pour the sauce over the chicken and serve.

YIELD: 4 servings

Turkey Sloppy Joe Bowls

* DAIRY-FREE * EGG-FREE * NUT-FREE

This hearty meal is made with pantry-ready ingredients (no processed ingredient packets here!) and my entire family loves it.

1 teaspoon olive oil

1 small onion, diced

1 cup (110 g) minced carrot

2 garlic cloves, chopped

1½ pounds (680 g) ground turkey

Salt and freshly ground black pepper, to taste

1 can (14.5 ounces, or 410 g) tomato sauce

½ cup (125 g) barbecue sauce

1 tablespoon (20 g) honey or coconut palm sugar, plus additional as needed

1 teaspoon Worcestershire sauce

½ teaspoon chili powder

Pinch of crushed red pepper flakes

In large skillet set over medium heat, heat the olive oil. Once the oil shimmers, add the onion, carrot, and garlic. Cook for about 4 minutes, or until the vegetables are tender and the garlic is fragrant. Transfer the vegetables to a bowl and set aside. Return the skillet to medium heat and add the turkey. Season it generously with salt and pepper.

Cook the turkey for 8 to 10 minutes, breaking up the meat with a spoon and spreading it around the pan. Continue to cook until the turkey is no longer pink.

Add the tomato sauce, barbecue sauce, honey, Worcestershire sauce, chili powder, and red pepper flakes. Stir to combine all ingredients.

Add the vegetables and stir to combine. Reduce the heat to medium-low and simmer for 15 to 20 minutes. Taste and adjust the seasonings, as necessary. If you find the sauce too tangy, add a bit more honey. Top with your favorite cheese, if desired.

YIELD: 6 servings

Laura's Tip

Serve over spiralized sweet potatoes or cauliflower rice (see method, page 145).

Chicken and Sausage Skillet Jambalaya

* DAIRY-FREE * EGG-FREE * NUT-FREE

The classic New Orleans dish is now revamped grain-free, but with all the taste of the original! A true cause for celebration at mealtime.

8 ounces (225 g) boneless skinless chicken breast halves, cut into 1-inch (2.5 cm) pieces

2 teaspoons Creole Seasoning (page 191)

Coconut oil, for cooking

8 ounces (225 g) cooked spicy or mild sausage, sliced

2 medium bell peppers (any color), cut into bite-size strips

1 small red onion, finely chopped

2 cans (14.5 ounces, or 411 g, each) no-salt-added stewed tomatoes, drained

3 cups (375 g) uncooked cauliflower rice (opposite page)

In a medium bowl, combine the chicken and seasoning and toss gently to coat.

In a large skillet set over medium-high heat, heat the coconut oil. Add the seasoned chicken and sausage. Cook for 3 to 4 minutes, stirring frequently, until the chicken begins to brown. Add the bell peppers and red onion. Cook for 2 minutes more, stirring frequently.

Add the tomatoes, breaking up any large pieces with a spoon. Stir in the cauliflower rice. Cover and cook for 5 to 7 minutes, or until the chicken is no longer pink.

YIELD: 4 servings

Chicken Sausage and Zucchini Noodles

* DAIRY-FREE OPTION * EGG-FREE * NUT-FREE

This is one of my simple skillet meals when this tired mom needs a break from the kitchen but the family still needs to eat.

1 tablespoon (15 ml) extra-virgin olive oil

½ of a sweet onion, chopped

1 can (14 ounces, or 396 g) fire-roasted tomatoes

12 ounces (340 g) precooked chicken sausage, sliced

2 large zucchini, spiralized

Soft goat cheese (optional)

In a large skillet set over medium-high heat, warm the olive oil. Sauté the onion for about 3 minutes, stirring often, until translucent.

Add the tomatoes with the juices to the skillet and stir. Add the chicken sausage and cook for about 5 minutes to heat through.

Top the sausage mixture with the spiralized zucchini, reduce the heat to low, cover the skillet, and simmer for about 3 minutes.

With tongs, toss to combine and serve. If you can tolerate goat's milk, top with a few crumbles of goat cheese (if using).

YIELD: 4 servings

How to Rice Cauliflower

* DAIRY-FREE * EGG-FREE * NUT-FREE

Cauliflower has a very similar texture to rice when you follow this method. It is a terrific substitute for the favorite grain in many dishes.

1 head of cauliflower

2 tablespoons (30 ml) oil, if cooking on the stovetop

To make the raw rice: Wash the cauliflower and remove the outer leaves. If you find any little black spots, remove them with a paring knife.

Cut the cauliflower in half, vertically, and then cut out the middle core. Discard the core.

Cut the florets into 1-inch (2.5 cm) pieces and place them in a food processor. Do not just turn it on and let it go, but pulse a few times until the cauliflower begins to break down. Continue pulsing until you have a rice-like consistency throughout.

To cook in a pan: Heat the oil in a pan set over medium heat. Add the cauliflower rice and any seasonings of your choice. Sauté until cooked through and soft.

To cook in the microwave: Place the cauliflower rice in a microwave-safe (glass or porcelain) baking dish. Cover with plastic wrap (if yours has a lid, use that), and microwave for 3 minutes on high.

Remove from the microwave, carefully lift the lid or plastic wrap, and stir with a fork.

Cover and microwave for 1 minute more. Test for tenderness, and season to taste.

YIELD: 4 servings

- -

KITCHEN NOTE

I like to freeze cauliflower rice in plastic freezer bags in 2-cup (200 g) portions. I freeze it before cooking. To use, remove the cauliflower rice from the freezer, thaw, and sauté as normal. After you freeze the cauliflower, the moisture content is higher so you may need to cook a little longer.

- -

Chicken in Spicy Peanut Sauce

* DAIRY-FREE * EGG-FREE * NUT-FREE OPTION

I first had this chicken when I visited Mexico City one Christmas nearly two decades ago. I watched our friends make this recipe from scratch and brought the recipe back with me. Over the years, I've simplified and adapted the recipe to become a quick skillet meal any family can enjoy.

6 bone-in chicken thighs, skinned if desired

Salt and freshly ground black pepper, to taste

¼ cup (56 g) coconut oil

½ cup (80 g) chopped onion

3 garlic cloves, minced

1 teaspoon ground Ancho chile pepper

1 can (14 ounces, or 396 g) fire-roasted diced tomatoes, drained

1 cup (235 ml) chicken broth

½ cup (75 g) dry-roasted peanuts, plus additional for garnish (optional)

1 teaspoon ground cinnamon

¼ cup (4 g) fresh cilantro

Cooked cauliflower rice (page 145), for serving

Season the chicken with salt and pepper.

In a large skillet set over medium-high heat, heat the coconut oil. Cook the chicken for 6 to 8 minutes, turning once, until golden brown and mostly cooked through. Remove the chicken and set aside, reserving about 2 tablespoons (30 ml) of oil in the skillet. Reduce the heat to medium.

Add the onion, garlic, and chile pepper to the skillet. Cook for about 5 minutes, stirring occasionally, until the onion is translucent. Transfer the onion mixture to a food processor or blender.

Add tomatoes, chicken broth, ½ cup (75 g) of peanuts, and cinnamon. Process with several on/off pulses until smooth. Return the mixture to the skillet set over medium-high heat. Add the chicken to the skillet.

Bring the sauce to a boil, reduce the heat to low, and simmer, uncovered, for about 30 minutes. Turn the chicken once, cooking until it's thoroughly done. The chicken should reach an internal temperature of 165°F (75°C).

Garnish with cilantro and additional chopped peanuts (if using). Serve over warm cauliflower rice.

YIELD: 6 servings

Laura's Tip

I use bone-in chicken thighs for this recipe because it yields juicer meat. Alternately, you can use boneless skinless thighs.

Allergy Substitution

Omit the peanuts.

Jamaican Pork Stir-Fry

DAIRY-FREE *EGG-FREE* *NUT-FREE*

Sweet, tangy, and really delicious and much healthier than takeout.

1 tablespoon (15 ml) oil

1 package (16 ounces, or 454 g) frozen stir-fry pepper blend

½ cup (80 g) sliced onions

1 pound (454 g) boneless pork chops, sliced into strips

1 tablespoon (5 g) Jamaican jerk seasoning

2 tablespoons (30 ml) coconut aminos

½ cup (85 g) pineapple chunks

Cooked cauliflower rice (page 145), for serving

Fresh chopped cilantro, for garnish

In a large skillet set over medium-high heat, heat the oil.

Add the frozen stir-fry mix and sliced onions. Cook for 5 to 7 minutes, stirring frequently, until the vegetables thaw and soften. Remove from the skillet and set aside.

Place the skillet back over medium-high heat. Add the pork and seasoning. Cook for about 5 minutes, stirring frequently, until the meat is no longer pink.

Add the coconut aminos and pineapple to the pork. Cook for about 3 minutes, or until the pineapple begins to release its juices and soften.

Add the stir-fried vegetables back to the skillet and continue cooking for 2 to 3 minutes more, or until everything is heated through.

Garnish with cilantro and serve with cauliflower rice.

YIELD: 4 servings

Kielbasa, Pepper, Onion, and Potato Hash

* DAIRY-FREE * EGG-FREE * NUT-FREE

This comes together quickly and leftovers make handy and hearty thermos lunches.

2 tablespoons (30 ml) olive oil

3 small or 2 large potatoes, peeled and diced small

Salt and greshly ground black pepper, to taste

1 onion, chopped

2 large bell peppers (any color), sliced

14 ounces (396 g) turkey sausage (kielbasa), cut into ¼-inch (6 mm) slices

In a heavy-bottomed skillet set over medium-high heat, heat the olive oil. Add the potatoes and season with salt and pepper. Panfry for 8 to 10 minutes, or until golden brown and cooked through, stirring a few times to ensure even browning.

Add the onion and cook for 3 minutes more, or until it begins to soften. Stir in the bell peppers and sausage. Continue cooking for 5 to 7 minutes, stirring frequently, until the potatoes are soft and the sausage is heated through.

YIELD: 4 servings

KITCHEN NOTE

Save time by using frozen peppers, typically sold as fajita peppers in the freezer section.

Chorizo and Squash Hash ▶

* DAIRY-FREE * EGG-FREE * NUT-FREE

This colorful dish is full of flavor and best complements a sunny side egg (or two) for a complete meal.

12 ounces (340 g) chorizo sausage, casings removed

½ cup (80 g) chopped onion

16 ounces (454 g) cubed squash

1 teaspoon garlic powder

1 teaspoon ground cumin

2 cups (135 g) kale, thoroughly washed, stemmed, and finely chopped

1 tablespoon (15 ml) fresh lime juice

Salt and freshly ground black pepper, to taste

In a large skillet set over medium-high heat, cook the chorizo for about 4 minutes. With a slotted spoon, transfer to a bowl and set aside. Keep the drippings in the pan.

Place the skillet back over medium-high heat, and add the onions. Cook for about 3 minutes, stirring often, or until golden and soft. Stir in the squash, garlic powder, and cumin and cook for 5 minutes more.

Add the kale and cook for about 2 minutes, or until wilted. Remove from the heat, stir in the lime juice, and season with salt and pepper.

YIELD: 4 servings

Laura's Tip

Save time by purchasing frozen cubed squash for this recipe. Simply thaw and incorporate into the recipe as directed.

One-Pot BBQ Chicken

* EGG-FREE * NUT-FREE

Incredibly delicious, this dish tastes like it takes a lot longer to make than it does and is a great midweek dinner. Use any chicken cut you like for this recipe. To keep things budget friendly, I typically use chicken thighs. The bacon is optional, but it adds a lot of flavor.

4 bacon slices, diced

1 pound (454 g) boneless skinless chicken thighs, cut into 1-inch (2.5 cm) chunks

2 garlic cloves, minced

1 onion, diced

¼ teaspoon crushed red pepper flakes, or more to taste

1 can (14 ounces, or 410 g) petite diced tomatoes

4 zucchini, peeled and diced small

⅓ cup (85 g) barbecue sauce, or more to taste

Mashed No-tatoes (page 200)

In a large skillet set over medium-high heat, cook the bacon until brown and crispy.

Add the chicken and cook for about 4 minutes, or until browned on all sides. Add the garlic, onion, and red pepper flakes. Continue cooking for about 3 minutes more, or until the onions are a translucent golden brown.

Stir in the tomatoes and cook the mixture for 7 to 10 minutes, stirring often.

Add the zucchini and reduce the heat to a simmer. Cook for 7 minutes, or until the zucchini is tender. Stir in the barbecue sauce. Simmer for a few minutes more, until the sauce is heated through.

Serve over Mashed No-tatoes (page 200).

YIELD: 6 servings

Papas con Chorizo (Potatoes with Sausage)

* DAIRY-FREE * EGG-FREE * NUT-FREE

One of my favorite quick sides or the base to a main meal topped with a fried egg.

1 pound (454 g) small new potatoes, washed and diced small

8 ounces (227 g) uncooked Mexican chorizo, casings removed

⅓ cup (50 g) chopped onion (about 1 small)

½ cup (90 g) chopped red bell pepper or yellow bell pepper (or a combination)

½ teaspoon ground cumin

Steam or microwave the potatoes until they are cooked tender.

In a large skillet set over medium-high heat, cook the chorizo for 5 to 7 minutes, or until cooked through, breaking it up into smaller pieces as it cooks. Remove from the skillet and set aside, reserving 1 to 2 tablespoons (15 to 30 ml) of the drippings in the skillet.

Return the skillet to medium-high heat. Add the onion, bell peppers, and cumin. Cook, for 5 to 7 minutes, or until the onions soften and are translucent.

Return the chorizo to the skillet and add the potatoes. Cook for about 3 minutes more, or until everything is heated through.

YIELD: 4 to 6 servings

Turkey Skillet Shepherd's Pie

* EGG-FREE * NUT-FREE

This is the classic comfort-food meal, made healthier and fast!

1½ tablespoons (20 g) coconut oil

1 pound (454 g) ground turkey

1 large onion, chopped (about 1 cup [160 g])

1½ cups (195 g) finely chopped carrots

2 tablespoons (32 g) tomato paste

1 tablespoon (15 ml) Worcestershire sauce

2 garlic cloves, minced

1 tablespoon (8 g) tapioca starch

½ cup (120 ml) chicken broth or stock

2 cups (260 g) frozen peas, thawed

4 cups (500 g) Mashed No-tatoes (page 200)

Chives, for garnish

In a large 12-inch (30 cm) skillet set over medium heat, warm the coconut oil. Cook the turkey and onion for 7 to 8 minutes, breaking up the meat with a spoon, until the meat is thoroughly cooked and the onions have softened. Drain off any excess fat.

Add the carrots, tomato paste, Worcestershire sauce, and garlic to the skillet. Cook for 7 to 9 minutes, or until the carrots soften.

Meanwhile, in a small bowl, stir together the tapioca starch and chicken broth and then stir the mixture into the turkey and veggies. Add the peas and stir to combine. Bring the mixture to a boil, reduce the heat to low, and simmer for 3 minutes.

Spread the Mashed No-tatoes over the top and simmer for about 3 minutes more, or until the potatoes are heated through. Garnish with chives and serve.

YIELD: 6 servings

- -

KITCHEN NOTE

Need to add starches to this meal? Make mashed sweet potatoes and substitute them for the Mashed No-tatoes (page 200).

- -

Pork Tenderloin Medallions with Strawberry Sauce

*EGG-FREE *NUT-FREE

This dish may sound fancy, but it is the best way to use strawberries that have been in your fridge for too long—and a tasty way to sneak more fruit into everyone's day.

For the strawberry sauce:

1½ cups (355 ml) reduced-sodium beef broth

2 cups (340 g) chopped fresh strawberries, divided

½ cup (120 ml) white wine vinegar

¼ cup (48 g) coconut palm sugar

¼ cup (60 ml) coconut aminos

3 garlic cloves, minced

For the pork medallions:

2 pork tenderloins (1 pound, or 454 g), cut into ½-inch (1.25 cm) slices

1 teaspoon garlic powder

½ teaspoon salt

½ teaspoon freshly ground black pepper

2 tablespoons (28 g) coconut oil

2 tablespoons (16 g) tapioca starch

2 tablespoons (28 g) cold water

½ cup (75 g) crumbled feta cheese, divided

½ cup (50 g) chopped scallions, divided

To make the strawberry sauce: In a large saucepan set over high heat, combine the broth, 1 cup (170 g) of strawberries, white wine vinegar, coconut palm sugar, coconut aminos, and garlic. Bring to a boil. Reduce the heat to low and simmer, uncovered, for 15 minutes or until slightly thickened. Strain the mixture and set the liquid aside, discarding the solids.

To make the pork medallions: Sprinkle the pork with garlic powder, salt, and pepper. In a large skillet set over medium heat, heat the coconut oil. Brown the pork for 2 to 3 minutes per side, turning to lightly sear and brown both sides. Remove from the skillet and keep warm.

Add the sauce to the skillet in which you cooked the pork and bring it to a boil. In a small bowl, combine the tapioca starch and water until smooth. Gradually stir it into skillet.

Return the pork to skillet. Bring to a boil and then reduce the heat to low. Cook, stirring, for 2 minutes, or until the sauce thickens and the pork is tender. Serve the pork with the sauce. Top each serving with about 1 tablespoon (9 g) of feta cheese, 1 tablespoon (6 g) of scallions, and 2 tablespoons (21 g) of the remaining 1 cup (170 g) of strawberries.

YIELD: 8 servings

Swedish Meatballs in Mushroom Gravy

* DAIRY-FREE * NUT-FREE OPTION

My first introduction to Swedish meatballs was many years ago in Europe at that very famous assemble-it-yourself furniture store. Clearly, I needed to make my own recipe at home. Serve with a side of Mashed No-tatoes (page 200)—or cauliflower rice (page 145) to keep it dairy-free—and a fresh salad and you're good to go.

1 pound (454 g) ground beef

¼ white onion, finely chopped

2 tablespoons (8 g) minced fresh parsley, plus additional for garnish

1 garlic clove, minced

¼ teaspoon ground nutmeg

½ teaspoon salt, plus additional to taste

¼ teaspoon freshly ground black pepper, plus additional to taste

1 large egg

½ teaspoon fennel seeds, ground

2 tablespoons (30 ml) oil

2 cups (140 g) sliced mushrooms

2 cups (475 ml) chicken broth

2 tablespoons (18 g) arrowroot powder

1 tablespoon (15 ml) cold water

1 cup (235 ml) unsweetened unflavored almond milk

In a large bowl, combine the ground beef, onion, parsley, garlic, nutmeg, salt, pepper, egg, and fennel seeds. With clean hands, thoroughly mix until all ingredients are combined and form 1-inch (2.5 cm) balls with the meat mixture. You should have about 25 meatballs.

In a large skillet set over medium-high heat, heat the oil. Place the meatballs in the hot skillet, working in batches if needed so you don't overcrowd the pan. Cook for about 10 minutes, turning a couple of times, or until they are deep brown all over and reach an internal temperature of at least 145°F (62.8°C). Remove the meatballs from the skillet and set aside, repeating as needed with remaining batches. Keep the drippings in the pan once done.

Return the skillet to medium-high heat and sauté the mushrooms. Once they have a nice sear, reduce the heat to medium, and pour the chicken broth into the pan. Scrape the pan to deglaze the bottom and incorporate the flavors into the gravy. Simmer for about 2 minutes.

Meanwhile, in a small bowl, whisk the arrowroot powder with the cold water. Stir the mixture into the skillet.

Pour the almond milk into the skillet and stir to combine. Season with salt and pepper.

Allow the gravy to simmer for at least 5 more minutes, until it begins to thicken. Add the meatballs to the sauce and simmer for about 5 minutes more, until heated through. Sprinkle with parsley and serve.

YIELD: 25 meatballs

Allergy Substitution

If dairy is not a concern, use regular milk. For a nut-free alternative, try hemp or rice milk.

Chicken Zoodle Soup

* DAIRY-FREE * EGG-FREE * NUT-FREE

Cut the carbs on your favorite soup by adding lots of veggies instead of pasta and this Chicken Zoodle Soup will become your new favorite homemade soup.

1 tablespoon (14 g) coconut oil

1 cup (150 g) peeled chopped zucchini

¼ medium onion, chopped

4 cups (946 ml) water, divided

4 cups (946 ml) chicken broth

¼ cup (32.5 g) diced carrots

¼ cup (30 g) diced celery

1 teaspoon granulated onion

½ teaspoon salt, or to taste

¼ teaspoon poultry seasoning

⅛ teaspoon ground white pepper

¼ teaspoon hot sauce

1 bay leaf

Pinch ground turmeric, for color (optional)

3 cups (420 g) diced or shredded cooked chicken

2½ to 3 cups (310 to 372 g) cauliflower rice (page 145)

In a large pot set over medium heat, heat the coconut oil. Add the zucchini and onion and sauté for about 4 minutes, or until tender. Transfer the mixture to a blender and add 2 cups (475 ml) of water. Blend until smooth.

Add the zucchini purée back to pot with along with the remaining 2 cups (475 ml) of water, the chicken broth, carrots, celery, granulated onion, salt, poultry seasoning, white pepper, hot sauce, bay leaf, and turmeric (if using).

Bring to a boil and then reduce the heat to achieve a low simmer. Cover and simmer for 10 to 15 minutes, or until the vegetables soften.

Add the chicken and cauliflower rice. Stir to combine. Heat through for about 5 minutes more, and season with salt before serving.

YIELD: 4 to 6 servings

Veggie-"Tortilla" Soup

*DAIRY-FREE * EGG-FREE * NUT-FREE

Try a bowl of this in winter and you'll soon be making it year-round! This soup is hearty, filling, and goes great with a Drop Biscuit (page 60). If you are not able to eat beans and legumes in your diet, add 2 more zucchini and omit the black beans.

2 tablespoons (28 g) coconut oil

1 large onion, chopped (about ¾ cup [120 g])

2 garlic cloves, minced

2 tablespoons (32 g) tomato paste

1 teaspoon ground cumin

1 teaspoon chili powder

½ teaspoon smoked paprika

¼ teaspoon salt

4 cups (940 ml) vegetable broth or stock

1 can (14 ounces, or 410 g) petite diced tomatoes, drained

1 cup (130 g) finely chopped carrots

¼ cup (4 g) chopped fresh cilantro, divided

1 can (15 ounces, or 425 g) black beans, rinsed and drained

1 large zucchini, chopped

1 avocado, peeled, pitted, and sliced

In a large saucepan set over medium-high heat, heat the coconut oil. Add the onion and cook for about 3 minutes, stirring frequently, until soft and translucent. Add the garlic and cook for 1 minute more.

Stir in the tomato paste, cumin, chili powder, paprika, and salt. Add the vegetable broth, tomatoes, carrots, and 2 tablespoons (2 g) of cilantro. Bring to a boil, reduce the heat to low, cover, and simmer for about 15 minutes to blend the flavors.

Add the black beans and zucchini to the soup. Cover and simmer for about 7 minutes, or until the zucchini is tender.

Ladle the soup into serving bowls, top with avocado slices, and garnish with the remaining 2 tablespoons of cilantro.

YIELD: 6 servings

Ramen Zoodle Soup

★ DAIRY-FREE ★ EGG-FREE ★ NUT-FREE

The classic "soup" from the foam mug has been reinvented with real and fresh ingredients!

2 tablespoons (30 ml) extra-virgin olive oil

3 garlic cloves, minced

½-inch (1.25 cm) piece of fresh ginger, minced (optional)

2 medium carrots, sliced

1 medium leek or 2 or 3 scallions (white part only), sliced

4 cups (946 ml) vegetable broth

1 cup (235 ml) water

2 tablespoons (30 ml) coconut aminos

¼ teaspoon salt

Pinch of freshly ground black pepper

2 zucchini, spiralized

In a large pot set over medium-high heat, warm the olive oil. Sauté the garlic and ginger for about 1 minute, or until fragrant. Add the carrots and leek. Continue to sauté for 3 to 4 minutes more, or until the leeks are translucent. Stir in the vegetable broth, water, coconut aminos, salt, and pepper. Bring to a boil and then reduce the heat to low. Simmer the soup for 5 minutes.

Add the zucchini noodles. Simmer for 3 to 5 minutes more, or until the noodles soften.

YIELD: 4 servings

Kale-Potato Soup with Bacon

*DAIRY-FREE OPTION * EGG-FREE * NUT-FREE

Like those "hearty" store-bought soups, but a lot healthier.

3 bacon slices, chopped

1¾ pounds (794 g) Yukon potatoes (about 3), peeled and diced small

1 leek (white and light green parts only), halved lengthwise and thinly sliced

2 garlic cloves, minced

2 teaspoons Homemade Italian Seasoning (page 141)

¼ teaspoon salt

4 cups (946 ml) low-sodium chicken broth

4 cups (946 ml) water

1 medium bunch kale, thoroughly washed, stemmed, and leaves chopped

¼ teaspoon Worcestershire sauce

1 tablespoon (15 ml) extra-virgin olive oil

Sour cream, for serving (optional)

In a large pot set over medium-high heat, cook the bacon for about 5 minutes, stirring occasionally, until crispy. Using a slotted spoon, transfer it to paper towels to drain. Keep the drippings in the pot.

Add the potatoes and leek to the drippings and cook for about 3 minutes, stirring, until the leek is slightly softened. Add the garlic, Italian seasoning, and salt. Cook for about 2 minutes more, stirring occasionally, or until the vegetables are lightly browned. Stir in the chicken broth and water and bring to a simmer. Cover and cook for 15 minutes.

Add the kale and cover the pot. Continue cooking for about 5 minutes, until the kale wilts. Stir in the Worcestershire sauce.

Serve the soup as is, thick and chunky, or purée it with an immersion blender or in a regular blender in batches. Top with the sour cream (if using) and serve.

YIELD: 8 servings

All-Meat and Veggie Chili

* DAIRY-FREE * EGG-FREE * NUT-FREE

This recipe continues to be one of the most-visited recipes on my personal website, LauraFuentes.com. It's hearty and full of flavor and veggies. It will soon become one of your go-to chili recipes, as well.

1½ pounds (680 g) lean ground beef

2 garlic cloves, chopped

2 tablespoons (30 ml) oil

1½ cups (240 g) diced onion (about 1 large onion)

1½ cups (195 g) diced carrots (about 4 medium carrots)

½ cup (50 g) chopped celery (about 1 stalk)

2 tablespoons (15 g) chili powder

1 teaspoon ground cumin

1 teaspoon dried oregano

1 teaspoon salt

¼ teaspoon cayenne pepper (optional)

3 large zucchini, diced

1 can (15 ounces, or 425 g) tomato sauce

1 can (15 ounces, or 425 g) diced tomatoes

In a large, seasoned cast iron skillet (5 to 6 quarts [4.7 to 5.7 L]) set over medium heat, brown the beef and garlic. Cook for 7 to 8 minutes, crumbling the beef while cooking, until it is cooked thoroughly and browned. Drain off excess any fat, transfer the beef to a bowl, and set aside.

Place the skillet over medium-high heat and add the oil, onion, carrots, celery, chili powder, cumin, oregano, salt, and cayenne pepper (if using). Stir to combine and cook for 5 to 7 minutes, or until the onions are translucent. Add the zucchini and cook for 2 minutes more, making sure to stir everything well.

Add the cooked beef, tomato sauce, and tomatoes to the pot and stir to combine well. Bring to a boil, stirring frequently, and then reduce the heat to low and simmer for 20 minutes.

Check on the amazing mixture every so often and stir. Serve immediately.

YIELD: 6 servings

- -

KITCHEN NOTE

This is a very thick chili recipe. Add up to 1 cup (235 ml) of additional liquid (tomato sauce or water) to thin out the sauce if you prefer.

- -

Laura's Tip

Watch how this recipe is made on YouTube.com/MOMables.

Butternut Squash Chili

* EGG-FREE * NUT-FREE

Thick, creamy, and vegetable rich, this chili satisfies year-round.

1 tablespoon (15 ml) extra-virgin olive oil

1 red bell pepper, finely chopped

1 medium yellow onion, finely chopped

2 garlic cloves, very finely chopped

1½ cups (360 ml) vegetable broth, plus additional as needed

16 ounces (454 g) butternut squash cubes cut into 1-inch (2.5 cm) pieces

1 can (15 ounces, or 425 g) white beans, rinsed and drained

1 can (15 ounces, or 425 g) whole tomatoes with juices, chopped into ½-inch (1.25 cm) pieces

½ cup (130 g) salsa or Homemade Salsa (page 66)

1 tablespoon (7 g) chili powder

1 tablespoon (7 g) ground cumin

2 teaspoons unsweetened cocoa powder

½ teaspoon ground cinnamon

½ teaspoon cayenne pepper (optional)

1 avocado, peeled, halved, pitted, and sliced

In a large soup pot set over medium heat, heat the olive oil for about 1 minute. Add the red bell pepper and onion and cook for about 5 minutes, stirring occasionally, until the onion is soft.

Stir in the garlic and cook for 1 minute more, until fragrant. Pour in the vegetable broth and heat for 1 minute, stirring and scraping any browned bits from the bottom of the pot.

Add the squash, white beans, tomatoes with liquid, salsa, chili powder, cumin, cocoa powder, cinnamon, and cayenne pepper (if using). Bring the chili to a simmer, and then reduce the heat to medium-low and simmer for about 30 minutes, stirring occasionally, or until the squash is tender and the chili beings to thicken. If the soup looks too thick while cooking, add additional vegetable broth to thin it out.

Top with avocado slices and serve.

YIELD: 4 servings

- -

KITCHEN NOTE

You can find frozen, cubed, butternut squash in the freezer section of many grocery stores.

- -

Laura's Tip

If you are not able to eat beans and legumes in your diet, substitute 2 zucchini, diced, for the white beans.

Slow-Cooker Sausage and Peppers

* DAIRY-FREE OPTION   * EGG-FREE   * NUT-FREE

Nicknamed "man food" by my husband Eric, this sausage and peppers meal is cooked in the slow cooker and is conveniently, and welcomingly, waiting to be served when we get home from work.

1 pound (454 g) smoked kielbasa sausage, sliced diagonally

1 pound (454 g) sliced bell peppers, any color (about 3)

1 large onion, sliced

1 can (15 ounces, or 425 g) diced tomatoes

1 can (15 ounces, or 425 g) tomato sauce

4 garlic cloves, chopped

1 tablespoon (5 g) Homemade Italian Seasoning (page 141)

2 tablespoons (32 g) tomato paste

¼ teaspoon salt

¼ teaspoon red pepper flakes (optional)

Place all ingredients inside a slow cooker. Stir to combine and cook for 6 hours on low. Serve over a baked potato (right) or cauliflower rice (page 145).

YIELD: 4 to 6 servings

Laura's Tip

We love to serve it with Drop Biscuits (page 60).

Slow-Cooker Baked Potatoes

* DAIRY-FREE   * EGG-FREE   * NUT-FREE

I prefer the "set-it-and-forget-it" method of cooking sweet potatoes or regular potatoes in a slow cooker. This method is quite practical, especially if you want to serve warm potatoes during the week.

3 to 5 medium sweet or white potatoes, your choice

Wrap each potato in enough aluminum foil to cover it completely.

Place each individually wrapped potato inside the slow cooker and cook for 8 hours on low, or 4 hours on high.

Remove from the slow cooker when you're ready to eat.

YIELD: As many potatoes as you put in the cooker!

Cochon-de-Lait Bowls

* DAIRY-FREE * NUT-FREE

This New Orleans–style pulled pork recipe is one you will make often. Traditional Cochon de Lait is made with a marinated young pig cooked outside in a pit … traditional, not practical! I've simplified the recipe to yield an effortless slow-cooker meal topped with a crunchy, tangy slaw.

¼ cup (48 g) coconut palm sugar

2 tablespoons (36 g) salt

2 teaspoons garlic powder

1½ teaspoons ground cumin

1 teaspoon paprika (smoked or regular)

½ teaspoon onion powder

½ teaspoon freshly ground black pepper

¼ teaspoon cayenne pepper

3 pounds (1.4 kg) pork shoulder roast

½ cup (120 ml) water

Creole Slaw (page 168)

In a medium bowl, mix together the coconut palm sugar, salt, garlic powder, cumin, paprika, onion powder, black pepper, and cayenne pepper. Transfer to a Mason jar or an airtight container.

Generously rub 3 to 4 tablespoons (45 to 60 g) of the dry rub on the roast and then place it in the slow cooker. Add the water and cover with the lid.

Cook for 6 hours on high, or 10 hours on low, or until the meat is so tender it pulls apart between two forks without resistance.

Thirty minutes to 1 hour before serving, remove the roast from the cooker and shred the meat with two forks. Place the shredded pork back in the cooker and mix with the cooking liquid. Simmer for 30 minutes to 1 hour more.

Serve over Creole Slaw.

YIELD: 8 to 10 servings

- -

KITCHEN NOTE

The rub mix should yield enough for 2 roasts. Store the leftover rub in a Mason jar, airtight container, or resealable plastic bag for future use.

- -

Creole Slaw

*DAIRY-FREE *NUT-FREE

This dish is one your family and friends will want the recipe for each time you serve it. It's a versatile side for many meals, but makes the perfect accompaniment to the Cochon-de-Lait Bowls (page 166).

2 bags (16 ounces, or 454 g) coleslaw mix

1½ cups (240 g) thinly sliced onion (about 1 large onion)

2 scallions, thinly sliced

1 cup (110 g) shredded carrots

½ cup (115 g) mayonnaise or Homemade Mayonnaise (page 68)

¼ cup (60 ml) white vinegar

1 tablespoon (11 g) Creole mustard or French mustard

1 teaspoon Creole Seasoning (page 191)

In a large bowl, combine the coleslaw mix, onion, scallions, and carrots.

In a small bowl, stir together the mayonnaise, white vinegar, mustard, and seasoning.

Pour the dressing over the vegetables and toss until the slaw is coated thoroughly in the dressing. Refrigerate until ready to serve.

YIELD: 6 to 8 servings

Slow-Cooker Salsa Chicken ▶

*DAIRY-FREE *EGG-FREE *NUT-FREE

The easiest way to pull off taco night—or any night you need a quick meal—guaranteed! Plus, cleanup is a breeze and the kids will cheer when these are on the menu ... what's not to love?

4 boneless skinless chicken breasts

2 cups (520 g) Homemade Salsa (page 66)

To a slow cooker, add the chicken and cover it with the salsa. Toss to combine and cover the cooker with the lid.

Cook for 4 hours on high or for 6 to 8 hours on low, or until the chicken shreds easily with a fork.

Shred the chicken in the slow cooker and toss with cooking liquid until everything is thoroughly combined.

YIELD: 6 servings

Laura's Tip

This recipe makes the perfect protein to tuck inside a Grain-Free Tortilla (page 124, and shown opposite), top a sweet potato, or add to a salad.

Asian Green Beans

* DAIRY-FREE * EGG-FREE * NUT-FREE

A restaurant in town has a side of Asian green beans I adore. With a hint of sweetness and touch of tang, this is my homemade version.

1½ pounds (680 g) green beans, trimmed

1½ tablespoons (23 ml) sesame oil

3 tablespoons (45 ml) coconut aminos

2 tablespoons (40 g) honey

1½ tablespoons (23 ml) apple cider vinegar

¼ teaspoon freshly ground black pepper

2 tablespoons (18 g) toasted sesame seeds

In a large pot of boiling water, cook the green beans for about 3 minutes, or until crisp-tender. Drain and transfer them to large bowl of ice water to cool. Drain them again and pat dry.

In a heavy large wok or nonstick skillet set over high heat, heat the sesame oil. Add the green beans and stir-fry for about 2 minutes, or until heated through. Add the coconut aminos, honey, cider vinegar, and pepper. Stir-fry for about 2 minutes more, or until the sauce reduces slightly and loosely coats the beans. Add the sesame seeds and toss to coat. Transfer the beans to a serving bowl.

YIELD: 4 to 6 servings

Carrot French Fries ▷

* DAIRY-FREE * EGG-FREE * NUT-FREE

Sweetly simple! Make veggies look like fries and all of a sudden they are more fun to eat.

1 pound (454 g) fresh carrots, cut into long, thick strips

2 teaspoons oil

½ teaspoon salt

Preheat the oven to 450°F (230°C) and line a baking sheet with parchment paper.

In a medium bowl, toss the carrots with the oil and salt to combine. Transfer them to the prepared sheet and place them in the preheated oven. Bake for 10 to 12 minutes, or until the thickest slices are crispy and golden brown on top.

YIELD: 4 to 6 servings

Laura's Tip

While this recipe is already quick to prepare, you can save even more time by preparing the green beans the day before. After cooking and cooling, wrap them in paper towels and enclose in a resealable plastic bag. Refrigerate until needed the next day.

Parmesan-Green Bean Fries

✶ EGG-FREE ✶ NUT-FREE

Tired of having green foods rejected at dinnertime? Serve these with some Homemade Ranch Dressing (page 74) for dipping and green beans have never been this fun to eat!

¼ cup (25 g) grated Parmesan cheese

½ teaspoon garlic powder

½ teaspoon salt

1 pound (454 g) fresh green beans, washed, ends trimmed

Preheat the oven to 425°F (220°C) and line a baking sheet with parchment paper.

In a small bowl, stir together the Parmesan, garlic powder, and salt.

Place the green beans on the prepared sheet, tightly grouped together but not laying on top of each other. Generously sprinkle the Parmesan mixture over the top.

Place the sheet in the preheated oven and bake for 12 to 15 minutes, or until the Parmesan has browned and the green beans are still crispy.

Remove from the oven and serve immediately.

YIELD: 4 servings

Green Beans with Sage and Mushrooms

* EGG-FREE * NUT-FREE

This simple side dish is often paired with a roast for Sunday supper.

2 pounds (908 g) fresh green beans, ends trimmed

Salt, to taste

2 tablespoons (30 ml) olive oil

2 tablespoons (28 g) butter or ghee

3 to 4 garlic cloves, thinly sliced

1 pound (454 g) large fresh button mushrooms

3 tablespoons (8 g) snipped fresh sage

Freshly ground black pepper, to taste

In a large covered saucepan set over high heat, cook the green beans in a small amount of boiling salted water for 3 to 4 minutes, or just until crisp-tender. Drain and immediately plunge the beans into ice water to stop the cooking. Let stand for 3 minutes. Drain and set aside.

In a 12-inch (30 cm) skillet set over medium heat, heat the olive oil and butter. Add the garlic and cook for about 1 minute, stirring just until golden brown.

Add the mushrooms and cook for 3 to 4 minutes, or until they begin to soften.

Add the green beans. Cook for 5 to 7 minutes more, stirring occasionally, until heated through. Remove from the heat and stir in the sage. Season with salt and pepper.

YIELD: 8 servings

- -

KITCHEN NOTE
Look for slender green beans that are crisp and brightly colored. Refrigerate them in an airtight container or resealable bag for up to 5 days.

- -

Cilantro-Avocado-Lime "Rice" ▶

* DAIRY-FREE * EGG-FREE * NUT-FREE

I can eat half of this recipe in a bowl, top it with a fried egg, garnish with some Homemade Salsa (page 66), and call it a meal; it's that good.

2 medium ripe avocados, peeled and pitted

¼ cup (4 g) chopped fresh cilantro

1½ tablespoons (23 ml) fresh lime juice

½ teaspoon ground cumin

1 small garlic clove, minced

Salt, to taste

Freshly ground black pepper, to taste

4 cups (500 g) cauliflower rice (page 145), hot

In a large mixing bowl, scoop out the avocado flesh and mash it.

Add the cilantro, lime juice, cumin, and garlic, and then season with salt and pepper.

Stir in the cauliflower rice, mix to combine, and serve warm.

YIELD: 4 servings

Garlic-Parmesan-Roasted Butternut Squash

* EGG-FREE * NUT-FREE

This is a staple side dish at most of our family meals. Leftovers make a great lunch the next day, too.

1 pound (454 g) butternut squash, peeled, pulp and seeds removed, and cut into small chunks

3 garlic cloves, minced

4 tablespoons (56 g) butter or ghee, melted

Pinch of salt

3 dashes of freshly ground black pepper

1 tablespoon (5 g) finely chopped fresh parsley

⅓ cup (33 g) grated Parmesan cheese (optional)

Preheat the oven to 350°F (180°C).

In a large bowl, toss the squash cubes with the garlic, melted butter, salt, pepper, and parsley. Transfer to a baking sheet and spread out the cubes in a single even layer.

Place the sheet in the preheated oven and roast for about 40 minutes, or until the surface becomes light brown and the flesh is tender and soft. Turn off the heat and remove from the oven.

Sprinkle the Parmesan cheese on top (if using) and put it back in the oven for 5 minutes, or until the cheese melts. Serve immediately.

YIELD: 4 servings

Maple-Roasted Butternut Squash

* DAIRY-FREE * EGG-FREE * NUT-FREE

This delicious vegetable is so versatile you can never have enough butternut squash recipes up your sleeve—especially recipes the whole family devours.

1 butternut squash, peeled and roughly cubed

Extra-virgin olive oil, for roasting

Salt and freshly ground black pepper, to taste

2 teaspoons finely chopped fresh herbs, such as thyme, rosemary, or sage

2 tablespoons (30 ml) maple syrup

Preheat the oven to 400°F (200°C) and line a baking sheet with parchment paper.

On the prepared sheet, toss the squash cubes with a generous drizzle of olive oil, a large pinch of salt, the pepper, herbs, and maple syrup.

Spread the cubes out into a single even layer and place the sheet in the preheated oven. Roast for 30 to 45 minutes, or until the squash is fork-tender and lightly browned.

YIELD: 4 to 6 servings

Laura's Tip

Use frozen cubed butternut squash. Thaw and toss with the seasonings. Roast for about 20 minutes, or until the tops are browned.

Sweet Potato "Tots"

* EGG-FREE * NUT-FREE

You won't believe how easy these are to make—and they're just like the ones sold in the freezer aisle, but with minimal ingredients. The kids will thank you.

3 cups (399 g) cubed sweet potatoes (about 3 to 4 potatoes)

1 cup (100 g) grated Parmesan cheese, plus additional for rolling the "tots" in

¼ teaspoon salt

Steam or boil the sweet potatoes to the point where you can pierce them with a fork but they're still too tough to eat. Drain (if boiling).

Preheat the oven to 425°F (220°C) and line a baking sheet with parchment paper or a silicone mat.

In a food processor, pulse the sweet potatoes and Parmesan a couple of times, just enough to break up the potatoes. Transfer to a bowl and fold over a couple of times. You want to have a chunky mashed texture just like the real "tots."

With a cookie scoop or your clean hands and a spoon, form the mixture into small balls. Roll each ball in Parmesan to coat it lightly. Place them on the prepared sheet.

Place the sheet in the preheated oven and bake for 12 to 15 minutes, turning at least once midway through to cook evenly on all sides.

Remove from the oven and serve.

YIELD: 25 to 30 "tots"

KITCHEN NOTE

To freeze, prepare the "tots" and place them on a parchment-lined baking sheet. Freeze for 1 hour and then transfer to a resealable freezer bag. To cook, just add a couple of minutes to the baking time called for in the recipe. Watch how these are made by going to "MOMables" on YouTube.

Allergy Substitution

I haven't been able to find a good substitute for the Parmesan cheese to make this fully dairy-free. Romano cheese is often made with sheep's milk, and it will work for this recipe. If you typically purchase a shredded cheese alternative, this recipe will work with it at a 1:1 ratio.

Spiralized Zucchini and Grape Tomatoes

* DAIRY-FREE * EGG-FREE * NUT-FREE

This spiralized dish is simple, fresh goodness. The playful twirls of zucchini on your plate will make you forget it's not really pasta.

1 tablespoon (15 ml) olive oil

2 or 3 garlic cloves, minced

16 ounces (454 g) cherry tomatoes, halved

1 teaspoon Homemade Italian Seasoning (page 141)

Pinch of red crushed pepper flakes

¼ teaspoon salt

3 large zucchini, spiralized

In a large skillet over medium-high heat, heat the olive oil. Add the garlic and toast for about 30 seconds. Stir in the tomatoes, Italian seasoning, red pepper flakes, and salt. Cook for 3 to 5 minutes, stirring often, or until the tomatoes begin to soften.

Reduce the heat to medium-low. Mix in the zucchini and toss to combine. Cover and simmer for 3 minutes, or until the desired doneness of the zucchini. Serve immediately.

YIELD: 4 servings

Laura's Tip

Spiralizing zucchini and other veggies ahead of time and storing them for the week is very simple. When you have veggies prepped to eat, eating grain-free can be even more convenient than taking a box of pasta out of the pantry.

All you have to do is spiralize the zucchini or veggies according to your spiralizer's directions. Refrigerate the veggie noodles in a paper towel-lined glass container, or resealable plastic bag, for 4 to 5 days. The paper towel absorbs excess moisture and the airtight container holds your veggie noodles for the next meal!

Cooking them is easy. Spiralized noodles can be sautéed lightly with a little oil and on your plate in a snap! This means that from the fridge to a meal can take less than 5 minutes. Spiralized veggies are the ultimate healthy fast food!

Cinnamon Butternut Squash

* DAIRY-FREE   * EGG-FREE   * NUT-FREE

The roasted sweetness of this butternut squash is so good you almost feel like you are eating dessert.

1 large butternut squash, peeled, seeds and pulp removed, and cut into 1-inch (2.5 cm) cubes

3 tablespoons (45 ml) olive oil

2 tablespoons (30 g) coconut palm sugar

1 teaspoon ground cinnamon

1 teaspoon salt

1 teaspoon freshly ground black pepper

Preheat the oven to 425°F (220°C) and place a rack in the upper middle position. Line a baking sheet with heavy-duty aluminum foil.

In a large bowl, toss the squash with the olive oil, coconut palm sugar, cinnamon, salt, and pepper until thoroughly coated. Transfer to the prepared sheet, spreading the cubes out in a single layer without overcrowding the pieces.

Place the sheet in the preheated oven and roast for about 40 minutes, rotating the pan midway through cooking. When the edges are browned and the cubes are fork-tender, remove from the oven immediately. Start checking the squash after 35 minutes, just to ensure they don't overcook.

YIELD: 6 servings

Smoky Cauliflower ▷

* DAIRY-FREE OPTION   * EGG-FREE
* NUT-FREE

When you overhear your husband raving about baked cauliflower to a friend, you know it's a dish worthy of including in a cookbook.

Butter or oil, for greasing the baking dish

1 large head of cauliflower, broken into 1-inch (2.5 cm) florets (about 8 cups [800 g])

2 tablespoons (30 ml) olive oil

1 teaspoon smoked paprika

¾ teaspoon salt

1 teaspoon garlic powder

Preheat the oven to 450°F (230°C). Grease a rectangular baking dish.

In a large bowl, place the cauliflower pieces.

In a small bowl, combine the olive oil, paprika, salt, and garlic powder. Drizzle the seasoning mixture over the cauliflower and toss to coat all florets.

Transfer the cauliflower to the prepared dish. Place the dish in the preheated oven and bake for 10 to 15 minutes, or until the tops are golden and the cauliflower softens.

YIELD: 6 to 8 servings

Sautéed Bok Choy

* DAIRY-FREE * EGG-FREE * NUT-FREE

This dish pairs beautifully with Asian-inspired meals such as the Skillet Teriyaki Chicken (page 142).

1 teaspoon coconut oil

½ cup (80 g) diced onion

1½ teaspoons grated fresh ginger

½ teaspoon sesame oil

1 teaspoon fish sauce

1 tablespoon (15 ml) apple cider vinegar

2 heads of baby bok choy, ends trimmed and sliced

3 tablespoons (60 ml) water

1½ teaspoons sesame seeds (optional)

In a large pan set over medium-high heat, heat coconut oil. Add the onions and ginger and sauté for about 4 minutes, or until the onions are translucent. Stir in the sesame oil, fish sauce, and cider vinegar.

Add the bok choy to the pan. Stir in the water and sesame seeds (if using). Cover and steam for about 4 minutes, or until the bok choy wilts.

Serve immediately.

YIELD: 4 servings

Lemon-Butter Broccolini

* EGG-FREE * NUT-FREE

If you are looking for a side dish that goes with everything, you've found it!

1 pound (454 g) fresh broccolini

3 tablespoons (45 g) unsalted butter

Zest of ½ of a lemon

1 garlic clove, minced

1½ tablespoons (25 ml) fresh lemon juice

¼ teaspoon salt

¼ teaspoon freshly ground black pepper

In a large pot of boiling water, blanch the broccolini for about 2 minutes. Drain immediately and transfer to a bowl of ice water.

In a large sauté pan set over medium-high heat, melt the butter. Stir in the lemon zest and garlic. Drain the broccolini and add it to the pan. Sauté for about 2 minutes, stirring frequently. Add the lemon juice, salt, and pepper and stir to combine. Cook, tossing, for 1 minute more, until the broccolini is heated through. Serve immediately.

YIELD: 4 servings

Laura's Tip

If you can't find broccolini, use regular broccoli for this recipe.

Baked Parmesan Mushrooms

* DAIRY-FREE OPTION   * EGG-FREE
* NUT-FREE

Easy sides that taste like they come from a restaurant are my favorite recipes to make when entertaining.

Coconut oil or cooking spray, for greasing the baking sheet

1½ pounds (680 g) cremini mushrooms, thinly sliced

¼ cup (60 ml) fresh lemon juice

3 tablespoons (45 ml) olive oil

Zest of 1 lemon

3 garlic cloves, minced

2 teaspoons dried thyme

¼ cup (25 g) grated Parmesan cheese

Salt and freshly ground black pepper, to taste

Preheat the oven to 375°F (190°C) and lightly oil a baking sheet.

Place the mushrooms in a single layer on the prepared sheet. Sprinkle with the lemon juice, olive oil, lemon zest, garlic, thyme, and Parmesan. Season with salt and pepper. Toss gently to combine.

Place the sheet in the preheated oven and bake for 12 to 15 minutes, or until browned and tender, tossing occasionally. Serve immediately.

YIELD: 4 servings

Allergy Substitution
Romano cheese is typically made with sheep's milk and can be used instead of Parmesan cheese (made with cow's milk). For dairy-free, use 2 tablespoons (10 g) of nutritional yeast instead of the Parmesan cheese.

Garlic-Portobello Mushrooms

* DAIRY-FREE OPTION   * EGG-FREE
* NUT-FREE

I first ate these mushrooms in Italy when I ordered the wrong item off the menu. To my relief, they were amazing and I've recreated the dish many times over since.

2 tablespoons (28 g) coconut oil

4 portobello mushrooms, gills removed and thickly sliced

2 garlic cloves, minced

Salt and freshly ground black pepper, to taste

¼ cup (25 g) finely grated Romano cheese

In a large skillet set over high heat, heat the coconut oil. Add the mushroom slices and cook for 5 to 7 minutes, stirring occasionally, until browned.

Reduce the heat to medium. Add the garlic and cook for 2 minutes more. Season with salt and pepper, and transfer to a serving dish.

Sprinkle the Romano cheese over the mushrooms and serve.

YIELD: 6 servings

Allergy Substitution
Make this fully dairy-free by omitting the Romano cheese.

Broccoli "Tots"

★ DAIRY-FREE OPTION ★ EGG-FREE ★ NUT-FREE

Have you heard? This is the newest way to get kids to love broccoli! Plus, these bite-size pieces will become a favorite, so make sure to prepare extras to freeze.

2 cups (220 g) russet potatoes, peeled and cubed (about 2 to 3 potatoes)

2 cups (142 g) chopped broccoli florets

2 cups (160 g) shredded Parmesan cheese, divided

1 tablespoon (6 g) Homemade Italian Seasoning (page 141)

Preheat the oven to 425°F (220°C). Place the oven rack in the middle of the oven and line a baking sheet with parchment paper or a silicone mat.

Steam or microwave the potatoes to the point where a fork is easily inserted but it's too tough to eat (about 10 minutes boiled, or 6 to 7 minutes on high in the microwave). Drain and set aside.

In a food processor, pulse the broccoli until it resembles coarse rice. Measure 1½ cups (106 g) of broccoli and transfer it to a large bowl. Reserve any remaining broccoli for another use.

In the processor, pulse the potatoes and 1½ cups (120 g) of Parmesan just enough to break up the potatoes and combine the ingredients. Add the mixture to the bowl with the broccoli. Add the Italian seasoning and fold all ingredients together with a large spatula to combine.

To a small bowl, add the remaining ½ cup (40 g) of Parmesan.

With a cookie scoop or your clean hands and a spoon, form the mixture into small balls.

Roll each "tot" in Parmesan, just enough to coat it. Place them on the prepared sheet, about ½ inch to 1 inch (1.3 to 2.5 cm) apart.

Place the sheet in the preheated oven and bake for 12 minutes, or until golden brown. Remove from the oven and serve.

YIELD: 6 dozen "tots"

Allergy Substitution

Make these dairy-free by omitting the Parmesan cheese. If you do this, make sure to press the "tots" together well so they hold their shape tightly.

Laura's Tip

Freeze unbaked broccoli "tots" on a baking sheet and transfer to a freezer bag once frozen. Keep frozen for up to 3 months. Bake as directed (no need to defrost), adding a few minutes on to baking time if needed.

Oyster Mushroom Chips

*DAIRY-FREE *EGG-FREE *NUT-FREE

My kids called these "chips" and the name stuck. They have a slight crispy texture and pair perfectly with grilled steaks.

1½ pounds (680 g) oyster mushrooms, stemmed and torn into bite-size pieces

Extra-virgin olive oil, for coating

Salt, to taste

Pinch of cayenne pepper (optional)

Preheat the oven to 375°F (190°C).

In a large bowl, toss the mushrooms with some olive oil until lightly coated. Season with salt and cayenne pepper (if using). Using 2 baking sheets, spread the mushrooms out in a single layer with no overlap.

Place the sheets in the preheated oven and roast for 10 to 12 minutes, or until brown and "cooked on" or stuck to the baking sheet. Remove from the oven and cool for 5 minutes. Use a bench scrape or sturdy spatula to get the mushroom chips off the bottom of the baking sheet. Transfer to a dish and serve.

YIELD: 4 servings

- -

KITCHEN NOTE

If you cook with bacon fat, substitute melted bacon fat for the olive oil to add natural flavoring to these chips.

- -

Sautéed Mushrooms and Bacon

*DAIRY-FREE *EGG-FREE *NUT-FREE

This recipe is super simple and, yet, it's named the best mushroom recipe by my husband.

4 bacon slices, chopped

1 tablespoon (15 ml) olive oil

1 pound (454 g) large fresh button mushrooms

1 tablespoon (11 g) Dijon mustard

2 tablespoons (8 g) snipped fresh Italian flat leaf parsley

In a large heavy skillet set over medium heat, cook the bacon until crisp. With a slotted spoon, transfer the bacon to paper towels to drain. Reserve the drippings in the skillet and maintain the heat.

Add the olive oil to the drippings. Add the mushrooms. Cook for 1 to 2 minutes, stirring, or just until they begin to brown. Cover and cook for about 8 minutes more, or until tender, stirring occasionally. Stir in the mustard. Heat for 1 to 2 minutes. Sprinkle with the crumbled bacon and parsley to serve.

YIELD: 4 servings

Creamed Spinach

EGG-FREE *NUT-FREE*

This classic side dish is delicious and perfect for days when you don't feel like eating "another salad" to get your daily serving of greens.

3 tablespoons (45 g) butter or ghee

2 tablespoons (16 g) tapioca starch

¼ teaspoon Creole Seasoning (at right)

¼ teaspoon salt, plus additional to taste

1½ cups (240 g) finely chopped onion (about 1 large onion)

3 garlic cloves, minced

24 ounces (680 g) fresh spinach

1 can (14 ounces, or 425 ml) coconut milk

Freshly ground black pepper, to taste

In a large skillet set over medium-high heat, melt the butter. Stir in the tapioca starch and cook for about 3 minutes, or until it's a thick paste.

Add the Creole Seasoning and salt and stir to combine. Stir in the onion and garlic. Cook for 3 minutes, or until the onion softens. Add the spinach and push it down into the pan so the heat wilts it.

Once the spinach begins to wilt, add the coconut milk. Mix thoroughly and simmer for 5 to 7 minutes, or until the mixture thickens. Season with additional salt and pepper, if needed, and serve.

YIELD: 4 servings

Creole Seasoning

DAIRY-FREE *EGG-FREE* *NUT-FREE*

A staple ingredient in my cooking, and a gift here from my kitchen to yours.

⅓ cup (37 g) sweet or Spanish paprika

3 tablespoons (9 g) dried oregano

2 tablespoons (12 g) freshly ground black pepper

2 tablespoons (4 g) dried basil

2 tablespoons (36 g) salt

1½ tablespoons (14 g) granulated garlic

1 tablespoon (5 g) cayenne pepper

1 tablespoon (7 g) smoked paprika

1 tablespoon (7 g) granulated onion

1 tablespoon (3 g) dried thyme

In a medium bowl, stir together the sweet paprika, oregano, black pepper, basil, salt, garlic, cayenne pepper, smoked paprika, onion, and thyme. Store in an airtight container for up to 3 months.

YIELD: About 1 cup (140 g)

Zucchini and Carrot Hash

* DAIRY-FREE * EGG-FREE * NUT-FREE

Quick, easy, and crunchy—that's just the start about what's great about this recipe!

1 tablespoon (14 g) coconut oil

2 garlic cloves, minced

2 teaspoons Homemade Italian Seasoning (page 141)

2 carrots, grated

Salt and freshly ground black pepper, to taste

2 zucchini, grated

In a sauté pan or skillet set over medium-high heat, heat the coconut oil.

Add the garlic to the skillet. Cook for about 1 minute, or until fragrant, and then add the Italian seasoning, carrots, salt, and pepper. Sauté for about 2 minutes, then add the zucchini. Sauté for another 2 to 3 minutes, or until it reaches your desired level of crunchiness.

YIELD: 4 servings

Brussels Sprouts with Bacon ▶

* DAIRY-FREE * EGG-FREE * NUT-FREE

This is the dish that won my husband over from his aversion to Brussels sprouts. It's a keeper!

4 thick-cut bacon slices, chopped

1 cup (160 g) chopped onion

1 pound (454 g) Brussels sprouts, bottoms trimmed, shredded

Salt and freshly ground black pepper, to taste

In a large skillet set over medium-high heat, cook the bacon most of the way through but not yet crispy. Add the onion. Continue cooking for about 3 minutes more, or until the onion is golden and translucent.

Add the Brussels sprouts and toss to combine. Cook for about 3 minutes, stirring often, or until the Brussels sprouts soften. Reduce the heat to low, cover, and allow them to steam for about 1 minute.

Season with salt and pepper and serve immediately.

YIELD: 4 servings

Root Vegetable Hash

* DAIRY-FREE * NUT-FREE

Top these roasted vegetables with a fried egg and call it a meal—breakfast, brunch, lunch, or dinner.

3 cups (450 g) turnips, peeled and roughly chopped

4 carrots, peeled and roughly chopped

2 medium beets, peeled and roughly chopped

2 shallots, peeled and chopped

2 tablespoons (30 ml) olive oil

4 large eggs

Preheat the oven to 400°F (200°C).

In a large bowl, toss together the turnips, carrots, beets, shallots, and olive oil. Spread them out on a baking sheet or in a large cast iron skillet (or two). Place the vegetables in the preheated oven and bake for 45 minutes.

If using a large skillet, crack 4 eggs over the nearly finished vegetables and place it back in the oven for about 3 minutes, or until the egg whites are set. Alternately, fry the eggs to your desired doneness and top each serving with 1 egg.

YIELD: 4 servings

Rainbow Slaw

* DAIRY-FREE * EGG-FREE * NUT-FREE

Colorful, crunchy, and not-your-average coleslaw. This will certainly help you "eat the rainbow" of color, nutrient-packed veggies today!

12 ounces (340 g) finely shredded cabbage

1 large red, green, orange, and yellow bell pepper, each thinly sliced

1 cup (150 g) sliced grape tomatoes

⅓ cup (80 ml) olive oil

⅓ cup (80 ml) white wine vinegar

1 tablespoon (20 g) honey

2 teaspoons dried basil

2 teaspoons dried oregano

1 teaspoon each, salt and freshly ground black pepper

In a large bowl, combine the cabbage, red, green, orange, and yellow bell peppers, and grape tomatoes.

In a small bowl, whisk together the olive oil, white wine vinegar, honey, basil, oregano, salt, and pepper until well combined. Pour the dressing over the vegetables and toss to coat.

Refrigerate, covered, until ready to serve.

YIELD: 8 servings

Laura's Tip

Prep this rainbow salad a day ahead of a party or gathering. It will have time to marinate and take in the dressing flavors.

Roasted Beet Salad with Walnuts and Goat Cheese

*DAIRY-FREE OPTION * EGG-FREE * NUT-FREE OPTION

This is the kind of salad you'll want to have a big plate of and call it a meal. While not everyone is a fan of beets, this dish could prove to be a game changer.

For the beets:

3 medium beets, washed, peeled, and cubed

1 tablespoon (15 ml) extra-virgin olive oil, divided

½ teaspoon Homemade Italian Seasoning (page 141)

¼ teaspoon salt

For the dressing:

¼ cup (60 ml) extra-virgin olive oil

2 tablespoons (30 ml) white balsamic vinegar

½ teaspoon Dijon mustard

1 tablespoon (15 ml) maple syrup

¼ teaspoon salt

For the salad:

4 cups (120 g) baby spinach

½ cup (75 g) crumbled goat cheese (optional)

½ cup (60 g) chopped toasted walnuts

Preheat the oven to 400°F (200°C).

To make the beets: In a 9 × 13-inch (23 × 33 cm) roasting pan, toss the beets with the olive oil, Italian seasoning, and salt.

Place the pan in the preheated oven and roast for 20 to 25 minutes, or until the beets are soft when pierced with a fork. Remove from the oven and set aside.

To make the dressing: In a medium bowl, whisk together the olive oil, white balsamic vinegar, mustard, maple syrup, and salt.

To assemble the salad: In a large serving bowl, place the spinach to form a bed for the salad. Top with the warm roasted beets and evenly distribute the cheese (if using) and walnuts over the top. Drizzle with the dressing and serve.

YIELD: 6 servings

KITCHEN NOTE

To toast walnuts, simply place chopped walnuts in a medium pan over medium heat. Toss the walnuts around so they do not burn, cooking for 2 to 3 minutes, or until fragrant.

Allergy Substitution

If dairy is not an option, omit the goat cheese. For a nut-free variation, substitute toasted pumpkin seeds for the walnuts.

Roasted Beets with Herb-Citrus Dressing

* DAIRY-FREE * EGG-FREE * NUT-FREE

Beets are high in vitamin C, folate, fiber, and essential minerals such as magnesium and potassium. Served warm or chilled this is one delicious way to eat this superfood year-round.

1½ pounds (680 g) beets, washed, peeled, and cubed

3 tablespoons (45 ml) olive oil, divided

½ teaspoon salt, divided

⅛ teaspoon freshly ground black pepper

Juice of 1 orange

Juice of 1 lime

1 teaspoon Dijon mustard

¼ cup (15 g) chopped parsley and basil or cilantro

Preheat the oven to 400°F (200°C).

In a 9 × 13-inch (23 × 33 cm) roasting pan, toss the beets with 1 tablespoon (15 ml) of olive oil, ¼ teaspoon of salt, and the pepper.

Place the pan in the preheated oven and roast for 20 to 25 minutes, or until the beets are soft when pierced with a fork. Remove from the oven and set aside.

While the beets cook, in a small bowl, whisk together the orange juice, lime juice, remaining ¼ teaspoon of salt, mustard, remaining 2 tablespoons (30 ml) of olive oil, and herbs. Set aside.

When the beets are done, cool them to room temperature and transfer them to a serving plate.

Drizzle with the dressing and serve.

YIELD: 4 servings

Laura's Tip

Toss any leftover beets with salad greens for a delicious lunch.

Mashed No-tatoes

* EGG-FREE   * NUT-FREE

A terrific way to eat more veggies in the familiar texture of mashed potatoes.

1 head of cauliflower, roughly chopped into 2- to 3-inch (5 to 7.5 cm) pieces (about 4 cups [400 g])

¼ cup (55 g) butter or ghee

½ teaspoon Homemade Italian Seasoning (page 141)

¼ teaspoon salt

Freshly ground black pepper, to taste

In the microwave or on the stovetop, steam the cauliflower until it is fork-tender. Transfer to a food processor and add the butter, Italian seasoning, salt, and pepper. Purée until smooth and creamy.

YIELD: 4 to 6 servings

Roasted Potatoes with Garlic Butter ▷

* EGG-FREE   * NUT-FREE

My grandmother would roast potatoes at the same time she roasted a chicken or any other meat in the oven. I have to say that oven-roasted potatoes are my favorite way of eating them.

8 medium Yukon gold potatoes, peeled and sliced into ⅛-inch (0.3 cm) thick slices

3 medium sweet potatoes, peeled and sliced into ⅛-inch (0.3 cm) thick slices

2 tablespoons (30 ml) olive oil

½ teaspoon salt

¼ teaspoon freshly ground black pepper

¼ cup (55 g) butter or ghee

3 garlic cloves, grated

1 tablespoon (3 g) minced fresh thyme or 1 teaspoon dried thyme

Preheat the oven to 425°F (220°C) and line 2 baking sheets with parchment paper.

In a large bowl, toss the Yukon potato and sweet potato slices with olive oil and season with salt and pepper.

Divide the potatoes between the prepared sheets and spread them out. Place the sheets in the preheated oven and roast for 17 to 20 minutes, or until tender.

Meanwhile, in a small skillet set over medium heat, heat the butter. Add the garlic and thyme. Cook and stir for about 1 minute, or until the garlic is fragrant and golden.

Once the potatoes are done, remove them from the oven and drizzle with the butter mixture. Toss to coat, if desired.

YIELD: 10 servings

Pecan Sweet Potatoes

★ EGG-FREE

I make these pecan sweet potatoes as our holiday side dish every year. I hope they find a place on your family table this year.

5 medium sweet potatoes, peeled and cubed

¼ cup (60 ml) olive oil

3 tablespoons (45 ml) white balsamic vinegar

½ cup (73 g) raisins

1 cup (160 g) finely chopped shallots

Salt, to taste

Freshly ground black pepper, to taste

2 tablespoons (28 g) butter or ghee

½ to 1 cup (55 to 110 g) pecan pieces

½ cup (120 ml) maple syrup

Preheat the oven to 350°F (180°C).

In a medium bowl, toss the sweet potatoes with the olive oil, white balsamic vinegar, raisins, and shallots. Season with salt and pepper.

Place the sweet potato mixture in a 9 × 13-inch (23 × 33 cm) baking dish.

In a skillet set over medium heat, melt the butter. Add the pecans and cook for about 3 minutes, stirring, until fragrant. Add the maple syrup and stir until most of the liquid is absorbed, about 3 minutes.

Top the potatoes with the caramelized pecans. Cover with the dish with aluminum foil and place it in the preheated oven. Bake for 50 to 60 minutes, or until the sweet potatoes are tender.

YIELD: 6 servings

Greek Pan-Roasted Asparagus

★ DAIRY-FREE ★ EGG-FREE ★ NUT-FREE

This is one of the simplest ways to prepare this elegant vegetable. The pan roasting brings out a slightly sweet and nutty taste, with a little zing from the olives and vinegar. Asparagus never tasted this good.

2 tablespoons (30 ml) olive oil

1 bunch of asparagus (about 1 pound [454 g]), fibrous ends trimmed and discarded, spears cut into 3-inch pieces (7.5 cm) pieces

¼ teaspoon salt

Dash of freshly ground black pepper

¼ cup (60 ml) balsamic vinegar

⅓ cup (34 g) pitted, chopped kalamata olives

In a large pan set over medium-high heat, warm the olive oil. Sauté the asparagus for about 8 minutes, turning occasionally, until they are tender and have browned in a few spots. Season with salt and pepper. Transfer to a serving dish and set aside.

Place the pan back over the heat and add the balsamic vinegar and olives. Deglaze the pan by bringing the vinegar to a boil and scraping the browned bits from the bottom. Cook the sauce for 1 to 2 minutes, or until it reduces by half. Turn off the heat and pour the sauce over the asparagus.

YIELD: 4 servings

Laura's Tip

If you can tolerate dairy, sprinkle the dish with crumbled feta cheese.

Pearl Onions, Peas, and Bacon

* EGG-FREE * NUT-FREE

The traditional combination of peas and onions, but kicked up that extra notch with bacon! My dad has the magical touch when it comes to cooking pearl onions. This recipe is almost as good as how he makes them, and that says a lot.

1 bag (16 ounces, or 484 g) frozen pearl onions

10 ounces (280 g) frozen peas

6 bacon slices, cut into 1-inch (2.5 cm) pieces

2 tablespoons (28 g) butter or ghee

1 teaspoon smoked paprika

1 teaspoon coconut palm sugar

Salt and freshly ground black pepper, to taste

In a large pot of boiling water, boil the pearl onions for 3 minutes. Add the peas and boil for 2 minutes more. Drain.

In a large frying pan set over medium-high heat, fry the bacon until crisp. Transfer to a paper towel–lined plate to drain.

Pour out most of the bacon grease, leaving about 1 tablespoon (15 ml) in the pan.

Add the butter to the bacon grease. Add the onions and peas to the pan. Sprinkle with the paprika and coconut palm sugar. Cook over medium-high heat for 4 minutes, stirring frequently. Season with salt and pepper, stir in the cooked bacon, and serve.

YIELD: 4 servings

Roasted Radishes and Carrots ▷

* DAIRY-FREE * EGG-FREE * NUT-FREE

A few years ago, I had a surplus of radishes in my farmers' box. Once I grew tired of eating them in salads, I experimented with other recipes. Who knew that roasting them brings out a slightly sweet flavor and makes them a lot more delicious?

1 pound (454 g) fresh radishes (about 1 bunch), greens removed and halved or quartered into same-size pieces

3 medium carrots, chopped into large chunks

2 tablespoons (30 ml) olive oil

2 tablespoons (30 ml) fresh lemon juice (about ½ of a lemon)

2 tablespoons (40 g) honey

Salt and freshly ground black pepper, to taste

Preheat the oven to 425°F (220°C).

In a large bowl, toss together the radishes, carrots, olive oil, and lemon juice. Season with the salt and pepper. On a rimmed baking sheet, spread the vegetables out in a single layer.

Place the sheet in the preheated oven and bake for 18 to 20 minutes, stirring once or twice during cooking.

YIELD: 4 servings

Grilled Pineapple

* DAIRY-FREE * EGG-FREE * NUT-FREE

Once you try grilled pineapple slices, you'll wonder where they've been all your life. They're so delicious you'll find ways to include them at breakfast, lunch, dinner, and dessert.

2 tablespoons (40 g) honey

1 teaspoon coconut oil

1 teaspoon ground cinnamon

Cooking spray, for coating the grill

1 ripe pineapple, cut into ½-inch (1.2 cm) thick slices

In a small bowl, whisk together the honey, coconut oil, and cinnamon. Set aside.

Prepare a hot fire in a charcoal grill or preheat a gas grill. If you don't have a grill, you can broil these in the oven.

Lightly coat the grill rack with cooking spray. Position the cooking rack 4 to 6 inches (10 to 15 cm) from the heat.

Lightly brush the pineapple with the marinade. Grill or broil the slices for 3 to 5 minutes on each side, turning once and basting once or twice with the remaining marinade, until tender and golden.

Serve warm.

YIELD: 6 servings

Mashed Turnips with Bacon and Chives

* EGG-FREE * NUT-FREE

Turnip dishes might not be found in many cookbooks but when your farmers' share box turns up with turnips for 4 weeks straight, you resort to cooking them in many ways! These mashed turnips taste like loaded mashed potatoes—almost. Plus, a 1-cup (150 g) serving contains 45 percent of your recommended daily allowance of vitamin C!

8 cups (1.2 kg) diced turnips (about 10 to 12 medium turnips)

Water or bone broth for cooking

½ pound (225 g) bacon

2 tablespoons (28 g) butter or ghee, melted

¼ teaspoon garlic powder

⅛ teaspoon onion powder

Salt and freshly ground black pepper, to taste

2 tablespoons (6 g) snipped fresh chives

In a large pot set over high heat, combine the turnips and water or bone broth. Bring to a boil and reduce the heat to a steady simmer. Cook for at least 30 minutes, uncovered, or until tender. The longer you simmer them, the better because they become less bitter. (Sometimes I let them simmer for more than an hour!)

In a skillet set over medium heat, cook the bacon until crispy. Transfer to paper towels to drain, reserving 2 tablespoons (30 ml) of bacon grease. When cool enough to handle, crumble the bacon and set aside.

Once the turnips are done, drain them well and return them to the pot. Add the reserved bacon grease, butter, garlic powder, onion powder, salt, and pepper. Mash to the desired consistency.

Fold in the crumbled bacon. Top with chives and serve.

YIELD: 4 to 6 servings

Fennel, Apple, and Celery Salad

* DAIRY-FREE * EGG-FREE * NUT-FREE

My mom makes this salad often and pairs it with grilled meats. This salad is for those of us who really enjoy the crunch!

2 large fennel bulbs

2 celery stalks, thinly sliced

1 large green apple, preferably Granny Smith, cut into julienne strips

Juice of ½ of a lemon

Extra-virgin olive oil, for drizzling

Salt and freshly ground black pepper, to taste

Slice the fennel bulbs horizontally into very fine shavings, preferably with a mandoline or food processor slicer. Place it in a large salad bowl.

Add the celery and apple. Drizzle with lemon juice and olive oil. Season with salt and pepper. Toss to coat well.

YIELD: 4 side servings

- -

KITCHEN NOTE

This salad can be made 1 to 2 hours in advance, if covered and chilled. The dressing prevents the apples from discoloring. Toss the salad well before storing it.

- -

CHAPTER 5
SNACKS AND TREATS

WHETHER YOU VISIT THIS CHAPTER for a little
snack-time inspiration or are searching for something
to celebrate with, many of these recipes will be the
most requested at your house, guaranteed.

Beet Dip

DAIRY-FREE *EGG-FREE* *NUT-FREE*

My daughter called this "the Barbie" dip for years and little did she know that this is one nutritious way to enjoy nutrition-packed beets!

2 large beets, washed, peeled, and cut into ½-inch (1.2 cm) cubes

1 can (15 ounces, or 425 g) chickpeas

Juice of 1 lemon

2 large garlic cloves, minced

2 tablespoons (28 g) tahini

½ teaspoon smoked paprika

¼ teaspoon red chili paste (optional)

½ teaspoon olive oil, plus additional if roasting the beets

¼ teaspoon salt

Place the beets in a double boiler and steam for 7 to 9 minutes, covered, or until tender when poked with a fork. Alternately, preheat the oven to 400°F (200°C) and place the beets on a baking sheet drizzled with a bit of olive oil. Place the sheet in the preheated oven and roast for about 15 minutes, or until tender.

In a food processor, combine the chickpeas, lemon juice, garlic, tahini, paprika, chili paste (if using), olive oil, and salt. Process until smooth and set aside.

When the beets are cool enough to handle, add them to the food processor and purée all the ingredients together. Refrigerate for 1 hour or until ready to serve.

YIELD: 6 to 8 servings

Lost-in-the-Woods Dip

* DAIRY-FREE * EGG-FREE
* NUT-FREE OPTION

"It's so good a big bear is going to steal it and eat it!"
Gabriel, age 3.

½ cup (125 g) Dairy-Free Ricotta Cheese (page 141)

½ cup (130 g) almond butter

2 teaspoons honey

Fruit (apples, pears, peaches), cut into wedges

In a medium bowl, mix together the ricotta, almond butter, and honey. Refrigerate for 1 hour and serve with the fruit.

YIELD: 8 servings

Allergy Substitution

If dairy is not a concern, use regular ricotta cheese or plain Greek yogurt. For a nut-free alternative, use sunflower seed butter or another nut-free butter instead of the almond butter and substitute sunflower seeds for the cashews in the Dairy-Free Ricotta Cheese.

Zucchini Hummus

* DAIRY-FREE * EGG-FREE * NUT-FREE

In the summer, when my parents' garden is overflowing with zucchini, we eat them in every way possible. This zucchini dip is a delicious alternative to traditional hummus.

2 medium zucchini, peeled and chopped

½ cup (112 g) tahini

⅓ cup (79 ml) fresh lemon juice

⅓ cup (79 ml) olive oil

3 garlic cloves

1½ teaspoons ground cumin

¼ teaspoon salt

In a food processor, combine the zucchini, tahini, lemon juice, olive oil, garlic, cumin, and salt. Process until smooth.

YIELD: 8 to 10 servings

Laura's Tip

Serve with crisp raw veggies, such as carrot or celery sticks, broccoli, cherry tomatoes, or cucumber slices for dipping.

Toasted Coconut Butter

*DAIRY-FREE *EGG-FREE *NUT-FREE

The whole family loves spreading this over slices of grain-free Blender Bread (page 40), on apple slices, or stuffing it into crunchy celery.

2½ cups (75 g) unsweetened coconut flakes

In a large skillet set over medium heat, toast the coconut, tossing it around the pan for about 2 minutes, or until light golden brown.

Once lightly toasted, transfer the coconut to a food processor. Process until smooth, about 5 continuous minutes, stopping a few times to scrape the sides of the bowl. After 5 minutes, you will have thick coconut clumps. Continue to process for an additional 12 to 15 minutes, or until you have a smooth peanut butter-like consistency.

If you use a high-speed blender, this process takes about 5 minutes.

Keep refrigerated in an airtight container for up to 1 week.

YIELD: About 1 cup (190 g)

Homemade Hazelnut Spread ▷

*EGG-FREE

You won't feel as guilty licking the spoon of this re-imagined sugar-free spread!

1 cup (135 g) hazelnuts

½ cup (120 ml) coconut milk, plus additional if needed

⅓ cup (105 g) honey

¼ cup (20 g) raw cacao powder

1 tablespoon (14 g) coconut oil

1 tablespoon (5 g) vanilla powder

Preheat the oven to 350°F (180°C).

Place the hazelnuts on a rimmed baking sheet and into the preheated oven. Bake for 8 to 10 minutes, or until brown. Transfer them to a clean kitchen towel (one you won't care if it gets stained!) and rub together in the towel to remove most of the skins, as they can be bitter.

Transfer the nuts to a food processor and process until smooth. Add the coconut milk, honey, cacao powder, coconut oil, and vanilla powder and process again until well mixed. If you want more of a "sauce" consistency, add extra coconut milk. Serve immediately and keep refrigerated for several weeks.

YIELD: 1 cup (260 g)

Plantain Chips

* DAIRY-FREE * EGG-FREE * NUT-FREE

I use these "chips" in any way you would use a cracker or tortilla chip. They are slightly salty, crunchy, and super delicious!

2 green plantains

1 tablespoon (14 g) coconut oil, melted

¾ teaspoon salt

Preheat the oven to 350°F (180°C) and line two baking sheets with parchment paper.

Cut the ends off the plantains and score the skins so you can peel them. Cut each plantain into diagonal slices, as thin as you can manage but keeping them similar in size.

Brush both sides of the plantain slices with coconut oil and place them on the prepared sheets. Sprinkle with salt.

Place the sheets in the preheated oven and bake for a total of 20 to 25 minutes, rotate and swap the baking sheets at around 15 minutes and flip the chips over. Bake for the remaining 5 to 10 minutes, removing the chips from the oven before they begin to brown.

YIELD: 5 to 6 dozen chips

KITCHEN NOTES

You'll want to use green plantains. Plantains are different than bananas in that they are larger, starchier, and not very sweet.

Beet Chips

* DAIRY-FREE * EGG-FREE * NUT-FREE

Roasted beet chips are earthy, sweet, and simply delicious when sprinkled with a little salt!

2 medium beets, washed and peeled

1 teaspoon extra-virgin olive oil

Salt, to taste

Preheat the oven to 350°F (180°C) and place two wire cooling racks inside two baking pans. This will lift the beets from the bottom of the pan and ensure even cooking and crispness.

Using a mandoline, slice the beets ⅟₁₆-inch (1.6 mm) thick. Transfer to a large bowl.

Add the olive oil to the bowl and toss the beets to coat. Distribute the beets evenly on the racks and sprinkle lightly with salt.

Place the beets in the preheated oven and bake for about 15 minutes, or until the edges begin to dry out. Rotate and swap the pans and flip the chips over. Bake for an additional 10 minutes, removing the chips as they become crisp and lighter in color.

Cool completely on the wire racks. The chips will crisp as they cool.

YIELD: 4 servings

Cherry-Chocolate Bites

* EGG-FREE * NUT-FREE OPTION

One bite and you'll be hooked on this delightful chocolate, cherry, cashew, chewy goodness.

1 packed cup (165 g) raisins

1 cup (137 g) cashews

½ cup (20 g) dried cherries

2 tablespoons (28 g) mini chocolate chips

½ teaspoon pure vanilla extract

⅛ teaspoon salt

In a medium bowl, combine the raisins with enough hot water to cover. Let soak for 5 minutes to soften, and then drain.

In a food processor, combine the soaked raisins, cashews, cherries, chocolate chips, vanilla, and salt. Pulse until the mixture turns into the consistency of sand. Remove the blade from the unit.

Using clean hands, scoop out the dough and form it into 16 balls between your palms. Place them on a plate.

Refrigerate for 30 minutes before serving. Keep refrigerated in an airtight container for 1 week.

YIELD: 16 bites

Apple Pie Bites

* DAIRY-FREE * EGG-FREE
* NUT-FREE OPTION

Bite-size apple pie without turning on the oven? Yes, please!

1 packed cup (165 g) raisins

1 cup (86 g) chopped dried apple rings

1 cup (120 g) cashews

½ teaspoon pure vanilla extract

½ teaspoon ground cinnamon

¼ teaspoon nutmeg

¼ teaspoon salt

In a medium bowl, combine the raisins with enough hot water to cover. Let soak for 5 minutes to soften, and then drain.

In a food processor, combine the soaked raisins, apple rings, cashews, vanilla, cinnamon, nutmeg, and salt. Pulse until the mixture turns into the consistency of sand. Remove the blade from the unit.

Using clean hands, scoop out the dough and form it into 16 balls between your palms. Place them on a plate.

Refrigerate for 30 minutes before serving. Keep refrigerated in an airtight container for 1 week.

YIELD: 16 bites

Allergy Substitution

Make the bites in these recipes nut-free by using sunflower or pumpkin seeds instead of the nuts.

◀ Coconut-Brownie Bites

*EGG-FREE *NUT-FREE OPTION

These are the one type of brownie bites I don't feel guilty eating at 4 in the afternoon when I need a quick pick-me-up.

1 packed cup (165 g) raisins

1 cup (120 g) cashews

¼ cup (20 g) cocoa powder

1 teaspoon pure vanilla extract

¼ cup (20 g) shredded coconut

¼ teaspoon salt

Pinch of ground cinnamon

In a medium bowl, combine the raisins with enough hot water to cover. Let soak for 5 minutes to soften, and then drain.

In a food processor, combine the soaked raisins, cashews, cocoa powder, vanilla, coconut, salt, and cinnamon. Pulse until the mixture turns into the consistency of sand. Remove the blade from the unit.

Using clean hands, scoop out the dough and form it into 18 balls between your palms. Place them on a plate.

Refrigerate for 30 minutes before serving. Keep refrigerated in an airtight container for 1 week.

YIELD: 18 bites

◀ Blueberry Muffin Bites

*DAIRY-FREE *EGG-FREE
*NUT-FREE OPTION

These have bite-size goodness without the guilt or grains.

1 packed cup (165 g) raisins

1 cup (120 g) cashews

½ cup (20 g) dried blueberries

½ teaspoon pure vanilla extract

⅛ teaspoon salt

In a medium bowl, combine the raisins with enough hot water to cover. Let soak for 5 minutes to soften, and then drain.

In a food processor, combine the soaked raisins, cashews, blueberries, vanilla, and salt. Pulse until the mixture turns into the consistency of sand. Remove the blade from the unit.

Using clean hands, scoop out the dough and form it into 16 balls between your palms. Place them on a plate.

Refrigerate for 30 minutes before serving. Keep refrigerated in an airtight container for 1 week.

YIELD: 16 bites

✴ Allergy Substitution

Make the bites in these recipes nut free by using sunflower or pumpkin seeds instead of the nuts.

Birthday Cupcakes

* NUT-FREE OPTION   * DAIRY-FREE

The original recipe for these cupcakes is located on my personal website, LauraFuentes.com, and has been visited a couple million times. I revamped the favorite chocolate cake recipe into cupcakes to be the ultimate recipe for any celebration.

½ cup (56 g) coconut flour

¼ cup (28 g) almond flour

1 tablespoon (9 g) Grain-Free Baking Powder (page 32)

½ cup (59 g) unsweetened dairy-free cocoa powder

4 large eggs

1 can (14 ounces, or 425 ml) full-fat coconut milk

½ cup (160 g) honey

2 teaspoons pure vanilla extract

Chocolate Frosting (page 220)

Preheat the oven to 350°F (175°C). Line muffin trays with 16 muffin cup liners. Parchment or foil liners work best; otherwise, grease or spray paper liners.

Into the bowl of your stand mixer or a large mixing bowl, sift the coconut flour, almond flour, baking powder, and cocoa powder. Mix together the dry ingredients until they are well combined.

In a blender, combine the eggs, coconut milk, honey, and vanilla. Blend on low speed for 10 to 15 seconds, or until all ingredients are thoroughly combined.

With your stand mixer or handheld mixer on low speed, slowly pour the wet ingredients into the dry. Mix just long enough for everything to combine. Stop the mixer once or so to make sure there are no dry ingredients left at the bottom. Do not overmix the batter. It should look like chocolate mousse.

Pour the batter evenly into the prepared muffin cups, filling them nearly to the top. Place them in the preheated oven and bake for 22 to 25 minutes, or until a toothpick inserted in the middle of a cupcake comes out clean.

Remove from the oven and cool the cupcakes in the pans for 10 minutes before transferring them to a cooling rack. Cool the cupcakes completely before frosting with Chocolate Frosting.

Keep refrigerated for up to 1 week.

YIELD: 16 cupcakes

Allergy Substitution
Use No-Nut Flour (page 32) instead of almond flour.

Chocolate Frosting

*EGG-FREE *NUT-FREE *DAIRY-FREE

You'll have a hard time not licking the spatula, and the entire bowl for that matter!

2 cups (436 g) coconut oil, refrigerated for 15 minutes to harden

1 cup (320 g) honey

1 cup (86 g) dairy-free cocoa powder

1 tablespoon (15 ml) brewed coffee

Make sure your cupcakes are completely cooled, or refrigerated for 15 minutes, before frosting.

In a food processor or blender, combine the coconut oil, honey, and cocoa powder. Add the coffee and process until smooth. If you blend it too much, the frosting will be liquid. Refrigerate it for 10 minutes to thicken if this happens.

Transfer the frosting to a piping bag and frost your Birthday Cupcakes (page 218). Refrigerate leftovers for up to 1 week.

YIELD: About 3 cups (860 g) frosting, enough for 16 cupcakes

Dairy-Free "Yogurt" Drinks

*DAIRY-FREE *EGG-FREE
*NUT-FREE OPTION

Like the store-bought ones, but with the goodness and nutrition of real fruit. Any berry will work great.

1 can (14 ounces, or 425 ml) full-fat coconut milk

2 cups (475 ml) unsweetened vanilla almond milk

2 tablespoons (40 g) honey

1 cup (255 g) frozen strawberries

In a blender, combine the coconut milk, vanilla almond milk, honey, and strawberries. Blend the mixture until smooth.

YIELD: 4 servings

Allergy Substitution

Use your nut-free milk of choice instead of the almond milk.

Banana Bread

*NUT-FREE OPTION *DAIRY-FREE

Banana bread seems to disappear at my house. It's a favorite breakfast food and sometimes I even use it to make almond butter and jelly sandwiches for lunch! What can I say; this classic recipe never gets old!

Butter or oil, for greasing the pan if needed

5 large eggs

1 cup (225 g) mashed ripe banana (about 2 large bananas)

6 tablespoons (84 g) unsalted butter or coconut oil, melted

¾ cup (101 g) coconut flour

½ cup (57 g) almond flour

⅓ cup (79 ml) coconut milk

¼ cup (80 g) honey

2 teaspoons pure vanilla extract

2 teaspoons Grain-Free Baking Powder (page 32)

1 teaspoon baking soda

½ teaspoon salt

Preheat the oven to 350°F (180°C). Adjust the oven rack to the middle position and line a 9 × 6 × 3-inch (23 × 15 × 8 cm) loaf pan with parchment paper making sure to grease any uncovered parts of the pan. This makes it easier to lift the loaf out of the pan.

In a food processor, combine the eggs, banana, butter, coconut flour, almond flour, coconut milk, honey, vanilla, baking powder, baking soda, and salt. Process until smooth. Pour into the prepared loaf pan.

Place the pan in the preheated oven and bake for 35 minutes, covered. Uncover the loaf and bake for 20 to 25 minutes, or until a toothpick inserted in the middle comes out with a few moist crumbs attached. Remove from the oven and cool the loaf in the pan for 10 minutes before lifting it out with the parchment paper. Cool the loaf fully before slicing.

YIELD: 1 loaf

Allergy Substitution

Use No-Nut Flour (page 32) instead of almond flour.

Apple Nachos

*DAIRY-FREE OPTION *EGG-FREE *NUT-FREE OPTION

These apple "nachos" are a delicious afternoon snack. For a treat, I sprinkle a few chocolate chips on top.

1 apple, thinly sliced with a mandoline

¼ cup (65 g) almond butter

2 tablespoons (6 g) unsweetened shredded coconut

Mini chocolate chips (optional)

Arrange the apple slices on a plate.

In a small microwaveable bowl, heat the almond butter in the microwave for a few seconds on high until it becomes thin and runs off a spoon.

Drizzle the almond butter over the apple slices and sprinkle with the coconut. Top with chocolate chips (if using).

YIELD: 4 servings

Allergy Substitution

For a nut-free version, use any nut-free butter instead of the almond butter.

Cherry Cobbler

*EGG-FREE *DAIRY-FREE *NUT-FREE OPTION

We are such fans of this recipe, I've even made it for breakfast!

Butter or oil, for greasing the pan

2½ cups (388 g) pitted fresh cherries
or frozen, thawed

2 tablespoons (30 ml) fresh lemon juice
(about ½ of a lemon)

2 teaspoons pure vanilla extract

1 cup (118 g) almond flour

¼ cup (30 g) chopped walnuts

¼ cup (60 ml) melted butter or coconut oil

2 tablespoons (30 ml) maple syrup or (40 g) honey

½ teaspoon ground cinnamon

Preheat the oven to 375°F (190°C). Grease a 9 × 9-inch (23 × 23 cm) baking dish.

In a large bowl, toss together the cherries, lemon juice, and vanilla until all the cherries are evenly coated. Transfer to the prepared dish.

In a medium bowl, combine the almond flour, walnuts, butter, maple syrup, and cinnamon.

Spread the nut topping evenly over the cherries. Place the dish in the preheated oven and bake for 40 to 45 minutes, or until the cherries are soft and the dish is bubbly on the sides.

YIELD: 6 servings

Allergy Substitution

For a nut-free version substitute No-Nut Flour (see page 32) for the almond flour and omit the walnuts or use ¼ cup (20 g) shredded unsweetened coconut instead.

Laura's Tip

If fresh cherries are out of season, use frozen cherries (thawed) for a year-round dessert!

Superfood Ice Cream

* EGG-FREE * NUT-FREE
* DAIRY-FREE OPTION

This ice cream has it all. It's nutrient dense, high in fiber, contains good-for-you healthy fats and fatty acids, essential vitamins, and antioxidants. This is one dessert you can feel especially good about serving.

3 ripe avocados

1 can (14 ounces, or 425 ml) coconut milk

½ cup (160 g) honey

¼ cup (84 g) cocoa powder

Scoop the avocado flesh into a food processor or blender. Add the coconut milk, honey, and cocoa powder. Blend until smooth.

Pour the mixture into an ice cream maker and freeze according to the manufacturer's instructions (about 15 to 20 minutes).

Serve immediately or freeze for later.

YIELD: 4 to 6 servings

Laura's Tip

If you don't have an ice cream maker, you can freeze the mix into ice pop molds.

Allergy Substitution

To make this dairy-free, use dairy-free cocoa powder.

Strawberry Soft-Serve ▶

* DAIRY-FREE OPTION * EGG-FREE
* NUT-FREE

My dear friend, Alison, shared this recipe with me this past summer and my family was hooked! If you cannot tolerate dairy, check out the Allergy Substitution note below.

2 cups (460 g) whole-milk Greek yogurt

½ cup (120 ml) maple syrup

1 cup (170 g) fresh strawberries, hulled and sliced, or frozen, thawed

In a medium bowl, stir together the yogurt and maple syrup. Gently fold in strawberries. Place the yogurt mixture into an ice cream maker and freeze according to the manufacturer's instructions (about 20 to 25 minutes). Serve immediately for a thick, soft-serve yogurt or freeze to harden further.

YIELD: 4 servings

Allergy Substitution

For a dairy-free version, substitute 2 cups (480 ml) full-fat coconut milk for the Greek yogurt.

Berry Macaroons

*DAIRY-FREE *NUT-FREE

My grandmother would make these for my aunt's birthday every year. They would disappear so fast, I'd have to beg my grandmother to let me eat one before anyone else came over to celebrate.

2 large egg whites

¼ cup (80 g) honey

1 teaspoon pure vanilla extract

2 cups (160 g) unsweetened shredded coconut

2 tablespoons (17 g) freeze-dried berries (such as strawberries or raspberries), crumbled with your hands nearly to a powder

Preheat the oven to 250°F (120°C). Line a baking sheet with parchment paper.

In a large bowl, beat the egg whites with a handheld mixer for about 30 seconds, until foamy.

Add the honey and vanilla. Beat on high for 4 to 5 minutes, or until stiff peaks form.

Gently fold in the coconut and berries, until just combined.

Scoop the batter by large spoonfuls onto the prepared sheet. Place the sheet in the preheated oven and bake 25 to 27 minutes, or until the tops are golden.

Remove from the oven and cool the macaroons to room temperature before transferring to a cooling rack to cool completely

Store in an airtight container for up to 4 days.

YIELD: 20 macaroons

Pineapple Whip Ice Cream

* DAIRY-FREE * EGG-FREE * NUT-FREE

This ice cream has a light and fluffy texture with the classic tropical combination of pineapple and coconut.

20 ounces (570 g) crushed pineapple (about 3 cups [495 g]), fresh or frozen

1 can (14 ounces, or 425 ml) coconut milk

2 tablespoons (30 ml) maple syrup or (40 g) honey

In a blender, combine the pineapple, coconut milk, and maple syrup. Blend until smooth. Continue blending for 1 minute, increasing the power to high.

Pour the mixture into ice cream maker and freeze according to the manufacturer's instructions. Alternately, you can freeze the mixture in a 9 × 5-inch (23 × 13 cm) bread pan for 4 to 6 hours until frozen. Use an ice cream scoop to serve.

YIELD: 6 servings

Almond Butter-Chocolate Chip Cookies

* NUT-FREE OPTION

Ooey, gooey, gone! Soon, these will become your family's favorite chocolate chip cookie, too!

2 tablespoons (40 g) honey

1 cup (250 g) almond butter

1 large egg

1 teaspoon pure vanilla extract

1 teaspoon baking soda

¼ teaspoon salt, plus additional for sprinkling

⅓ cup (58 g) chocolate chips

Preheat the oven to 350°F (180°C). Line a large baking sheet with parchment paper or a silicone baking mat. Set aside.

In a medium bowl, mix together the honey and almond butter until creamy and smooth. Add the egg and vanilla. Mix again until well combined.

Stir in the baking soda, ¼ teaspoon of salt, and chocolate chips.

Shape the dough into 15 small balls. The dough will be a little crumbly, but just squeeze it together. Place them on the prepared sheet about 2 inches (5 cm) apart. Sprinkle with salt.

Place the sheet in the preheated oven and bake cookies for 8 to 10 minutes or until they start to brown around the edges. Don't over bake. Let the cookies sit on the baking sheet for 2 to 3 minutes. Transfer to a wire rack to cool completely.

YIELD: 15 cookies

Allergy Substitution

For a nut-free version, use 1 cup (250 g) sunflower seed butter instead of the almond butter.

ACKNOWLEDGMENTS

To Eric, my best friend, husband, and love of my life. For letting me write "just one more book" so I could share our favorite recipes with many families. I appreciate you understanding that sharing these special diet recipes can be life-changing for many families. Your support and encouragement are two of the biggest gifts of my life.

To my kids Sofia, Alex, and Gabriel. I know you don't always like what mom cooks or when she tests recipes, so I thank you for at least doing the "taste test" and listening to mom's mantra: We might not like this recipe today, but tomorrow we might discover a new favorite.

To my parents, John and Isabel. There are no words that can describe how much I love you.

My in-laws, Moose and Debbie. You are the most amazing, caring, and loving in-laws I could ever ask for. Your help in taking care of the kids so I can finish this book has been a gift.

My MOMables team. You are amazing. Truly. Thank you for knowing when to step in when I've left off test recipes and for when I work on cookbooks, travel, and have to be mom and disappear off of the radar for a week or so.

My friend Alison Bickel. The third time is the charm. Thank you for having an awesome hungry family that continues to eat my recipes after you photograph them. I still believe that you are able to capture with a camera even better than how I see food in my mind so I can share it with others.

To Amanda, my editor, and the publishing team. These three books have been a great journey. Betsy, you'll be missed tremendously.

To our Creator. With you, all things are possible.

ABOUT THE AUTHOR

Laura Fuentes is the founder and CEO of MOMables.com, where she helps thousands of parents every day make meals their kids will love.

Laura is the author of *The Best Homemade Kids' Lunches on the Planet* and *The Best Homemade Kids' Snacks on the Planet*. She is a regular contributor to numerous print magazines, *TODAY*, the *Huffington Post*, and other online publications.

Laura's passion for teaching parents how to make fresh meals expands beyond print into video. She's competed on the Food Network (and won!), appeared on TODAY, and regularly shares cooking videos on her YouTube Channel, http://YouTube.com/MOMables.

In her personal blog, Laura writes about motherhood, good family food, managing deadlines, and keeping her cool, even when her kids super-glued her hair.

Above all, her most important job is caring for her family.

To find out more about Laura, visit www.LauraFuentes.com.

Index